AROUND MOLD
ODDI AMGYLCH YR WYDDGRUG

DAVID ROWE

The History Press

First published in 2008 by
The History Press
The Mill, Brimscombe Port,
Stroud, Gloucestershire, GL5 2QG
www.thehistorypress.co.uk

Reprinted in 2008, 2010, 2011, 2012

British Library Cataloguing in Publication Data
A catalogue record for this book is available from the British Library.

ISBN 978 0 7509 4947 7

To my long-suffering wife Judith, and those volunteers throughout the world who give up countless hours to record and preserve our heritage.

Mold Urban District Council adopted the town crest in 1895. It consists of a lion rampant quartered with the Prince of Wales Feathers. The symbol on top of the shield is a baron's crown showing that Mold is a baronetcy and the motto translates roughly to 'Safe is the owner of a clear conscience'. *(Rhiannon Griffiths)*

Typesetting and origination by
The History Press.
Printed and bound in England.

CONTENTS

Introduction   4

Some Thoughts on Mold   8

1.   Historic Events   9

2.   High Street   15

3.   Churches & Chapels   23

4.   Commerce   31

5.   Hotels & Pubs   45

6.   Houses   53

7.   Industry   67

8.   Sport & Leisure   77

9.   People   89

10.   Public Service   97

11.   Schools   109

12.   Transport   115

13.   Market Day   123

Acknowledgements   127

INTRODUCTION

Almost thirty years ago I visited North East Wales on a business trip from my native Tyneside and was struck by the natural beauty of the area along with the friendliness of the local people. From the Clwyd Gate Inn, the view of the Vale of Clwyd and the beauty of the tree-lined road from Denbigh to Mold remained etched in my memory, so, six years later when I was offered a job at Deeside, I had no hesitation in taking the position and chose to live in Wales rather than Cheshire, which proved to be one of my better life decisions.

Although my working life has taken me to a variety of overseas locations, the Mold area always remained my home and I fully subscribe to the Welsh word 'hiraeth', which translates as longing.

This book is a personal journey and my way of saying thank you to all the friends my family and I have made over the last twenty-three years, and hopefully we have appreciated the culture and language of what is a unique area.

So what makes the Mold area so special? It is, first and foremost, a border town, and therefore experienced constant warfare for many centuries but, as conflict lessened and the population became more settled, the Welsh and English lived in harmony – though this is not always apparent during the Six Nations Rugby Union internationals.

The nearby Clwydian hills contain a number of hill forts that are a testament to early dwellers, although traces of other civilisations are evident from excavated cave dwellings and the magnificent Mold Gold Cape.

The Romans are known to have mined in the area but in general have not left a legacy in the immediate Mold vicinity. The next major event, as recorded by Bede in the Anglo-Saxon Chronicles, is the Alleliua Battle fought at Maes Garmon just outside Mold, and details of this are given elsewhere in the book.

The coming of the Normans brought Mold into the spotlight and the Montalt family built a motte and bailey castle on what we now know as Bailey Hill. This was the scene of a number of battles, one of which is described on page 10.

Following the victory of Henry Tudor over Richard III at Bosworth Field, Henry's mother, Margaret Beaufort, sponsored the building of St Mary's Church and while this is much altered, it, along with Bailey Hill, still dominate the town.

The town saw a little action during the Civil War, generally in the form of minor skirmishes with the local gentry who, in the main, remained loyal to the king. In the High Street you will observe the original portico of the old Black Lion Hotel, a building that played a part in the downfall of Hitler, with British Intelligence enacting a plan to deceive Germany as to the Allies' invasion plans. The story of the master plan was the subject of the 1956 film *The Man who Never Was* starring Clifton Webb.

Some invasions of the area have brought benefits such as the influx of labour in the 1800s to work in the many mines (metal and coal), brickworks, potteries and other such industries. These included workers from Ireland, Durham, Newcastle, Derbyshire, Cornwall and Staffordshire and a large Italian community remains a fixture throughout the area. Many of these early workers remained and left a permanent legacy, as evidenced by the unique Staffordshire/Welsh dialect of the nearby town of Buckley.

This industrial migration from England was not without its problems. The Welsh language disappeared from previously Welsh-speaking areas; the area was predominately non-conformist while many of the incomers and landowners were Anglican, leading to disputes in educational and religious matters. An 1847 report of Anglican Commissioners was very scathing about the Welsh language, concluding that ignorance of English was synonymous with illiteracy and Welsh was 'a barrier to moral progress, pandering to prevarication and perjury, if not worse'. In addition, the colliery and mine managers were often English and this was a factor in some serious rioting, culminating in the deaths of four people in what became known as the Mold Riots in 1869.

The use of Welsh is now on the increase, particularly among young people, and the fact that the 2007 National Eisteddfod was held in Mold should mean that the language and cultural traditions will receive a further boost

Mold, like many towns throughout England and Wales, has seen the role of the High Street changing and while we also have a surfeit of charity shops, Mold has retained many of its traditional businesses, its cattle market and a street market that is still held on Wednesdays and Saturdays.

Restaurants of many types abound, and 2006 saw the inaugural annual Food and Drink Festival showcasing local produce and attracting visitors from throughout the area. The town has now obtained 'Cittaslow' status. In addition, the area offers a wide range of sporting and other recreational activities within the locality and these, as has been the case over the centuries, draw many visitors. The town library in the Daniel Owen Civic Square has a small museum that provides a wonderful insight into the history and personalities of Mold.

Mold & District Civic Society runs a series of lectures, promotes the blue plaque scheme, publishes an annual journal, *Ystrad Alun*, and has produced a CD-ROM containing over 1,600 images of Mold and District. If you wish to learn more about the work of the society or obtain copies of their publications, please contact the author at: david@daverowe.co.uk or Mrs Diane Johnson at: typedwar@tiscali.co.uk

I hope you enjoy my personal journey. There were so many other aspects I could have looked at but space did not permit. However, if you are a resident, hopefully you will have discovered something new about this ancient market town, and if you have never visited, please don't leave it too long before you do.

David Rowe

CYFLWYNIAD

Ymwelais â gogledd-ddwyrain Cymru o'm cartref ar Lannau Tyne am y tro cyntaf tua trideg mlynedd yn ôl, a hynny yn rinwedd fy swydd. Gwirionais yn syth ar gyfeillgarwch y bobl a harddwch yr ardal. Yn ddi-os, yr olygfa a wnaeth yr argraff fwyaf arnaf oedd yr un a geir wrth droi'r gornel yn Adwy Clwyd a dod wyneb yn wyneb ag ysblander panoramig Dyffryn Clwyd, hefyd, y coed godidog a geir ar y naill ochr i'r ffordd ar llall o'r Wyddgrug i Ddinbych. Felly, pan gynhigiwyd swydd i mi ar Lannau Dyfrdwy chwe blynedd yn ddiweddarach derbyniais heb feddwl eilwaith gan ddewis byw yng Nghymru yn hytrach na thros y ffin; un o'r penderfyniadau gorau a wnes erioed. Yn wir, er i'm gwaith fy ngalluogi i ymweld yn gyson â gwledydd pell, Yr Wyddgrug yw fy nghartref bellach a phan oddi yno byddaf yn deall y gair *hiraeth.*

Siwrnai bersonol yw'r llyfr hwn a fy ffordd i a ffordd fy nheulu o ddangos ein gwerthfawrogiad am ddauddeg-tri o flynyddoedd mewn ardal ble mae ddiwylliant ag iaith arbennig. Felly, beth sy mor unigryw am ardal Yr Wyddgrug?

Yn gyntaf, mae'n dref hynafol yn ffinio â Lloegr ac wedi gwrthsefyll llawer i frwydr erchyll dros y canrifoedd, ond wedi i'r rhyfeloedd ostegu ymsefydlodd y Cymry a'r Saeson yn gytun yma, hynny yw, ar wahân i adeg gemau Rygbi Rhyngwladol y Chwe Gwlad!

Dywed y caerau hynafol a welir ar gopaon Bryniau Clwyd wrthym i bobl yr Oes Haearn (600 C.C – 600 O.C.) breswylio ar yr ucheldir gerllaw filoedd o flynyddoedd yn ôl, tra bo'r clogyn aur (1500 C.C.) a ddarganfuwyd yn Yr Wyddgrug yn brawf pendant fod y safle hwnnw'n ganolfan bwysig yn ystod yr Oes Efydd. Yn wir, cawn dystiolaeth archaeolegol fod dyn cyntefig wedi defnyddio'r ogofâu yn y cyffiniau ymhell cyn hynny.

Er i'r Rhufeiniad gloddio am blwm yn y tiroedd cyfagos ni adawsant eu hôl yma ac mae'n rhaid aros tan i'r Hybarch Beda ysgrifennu ei *Hanes Eglwysig* cyn y clywn am ddigwyddiad penodol, sef, 'Brwydr Aleliwia'(429 O.C.), a gymerodd le ar dir Maes Garmon; dafliad carreg oddi allan i'r dref i gyfeiriad Y Waun. Ceir manylion o'r digwyddiad ymhellach ymlaen.

Ymsefydlodd y Normaniaid yn y fro yn niwedd yr unfed ganrif ar ddeg, gan godi tomen-a-beili ar fryncyn o'r enw Yr Wyddgrug. Y teulu a fu'n gyfrifol oedd y Mohatiaid; wedi cymeryd eu henw oddi wrth y *Mont-hault* 'bryn uchel' roeddynt wedi codi eu amddiffynfa arno, yr hwn a elwir heddiw yn Bryn-y-beili. Bu amryw frwydrau yno a disgrifir un ohonynt ar dudalen 10. Mae'r Bryn i'w weld yn glir o bell, ac ar ei ochr ddeheuol ceir Eglwys Santes Fair a godwyd *c.* 1495–1520 drwy gymorth ariannol gan Margaret Beaufort (gwraig Arglwydd y Faenor a mam y brenin Harri Tudur). Bu llawer o newidiadau i'r adeilad ers hynny ond mae'n dal i edrych yn ogoneddus o ba gyfeiriad bynnag yr edrychir arno.

Arhosodd yr uchelwyr lleol, fwy neu lai, yn driw i'r Brennin yn ystod y Rhyfel Cartref a'r unig helynt a welwyd oedd sgarmes fechan ar dir Gwysaneu.

Yn y Stryd Fawr gellir gweld portico gwreiddiol gwesty'r Llew Du nad yw'n dafarn mwyach. Yr oedd yn adeilad a chwaraeodd ran bychan, ond o bosib pwysig, yng nghwymp Hitler yn ystod yr Ail Ryfel Byd gan i Wasanaeth-cudd Prydain gyfeirio ato wrth gynllwynio i dwyllo'r Almaen yngl n â bwriad y Gynghreiriad i ymosod ar Ewrob. Fe fu'r twyll yn un llwyddiannus a gwnaethpwyd ffilm o'r stori: *The Man Who Never Was.*

Bu cyfran sylweddol o'r newydd-ddyfodiaid a ddaeth i'r ardal, yn enwedig o 1800 ymlaen, yn gymorth mawr i ddatblygu'r ardal yn gyffredinol. Yn ogystal â gw r a gwragedd o Gymru a'r Gororau, ceid rhai o Swydd Derby, Cernyw a phellteroedd Durham a Newcastle. Dywedir i acen neilltuol Bwcle fod yn gyfuniad o'r Gymraeg a thafodiaith Swydd Stafford.

Daeth y mewnlifiad yma o Saeson â phroblemau yn ei sgil. Y mwyaf brawychys oedd i'r iaith Gymraeg ddiflannu o lawer i dref a phentre a oedd gynt yn hollol Gymreig. Yn ychwanegol, Anglicaniaid oedd y rhelyw o'r dieithriaid a bu gwrthdaro rhyngddynt a'r ymneilltuwyr lleol. Aeth pethau'n ddrwg iawn ar ôl cyhoeddi Adroddiad y Comisiynwyr Anglicanaidd ar gyflwr ysgolion Cymru ym 1847, a lys-enwyd yn 'Brad y Llyfrau Gleision'. Datganodd y gwybodusion fod anwybodaeth o'r Saesneg yn gyfystyr â bod yn anllythrennog a gwelsant y Gymraeg yn *barrier to moral progress, pandering to prevarication and perjury, if not worse'*. Nid syndod felly yw darganfod i lawer o reolwyr y mwyngloddiau a phyllau glo fod yn uniaith-Saesneg; un o'r rhesymau i derfysg dorri allan yn Yr Wyddgrug ym 1869, ble cafodd pedwar diniwed o'r dorf eu lladd yn ddamweiniol gan filwyr.

Yn ddiweddar mae'r Gymraeg ar gynnydd, yn enwedig ymysg y bobl ifanc, ac fe adlewyrchir hyn yn y ffaith i Eisteddfod Yr Urdd ymweld â'r dref ym 1984, a'r Eisteddfod Genedlaethol yn 1991, ac eto yn 2007; achlysuron a fu'n gyfrifol am godi proffil yr iaith a gwneud y trigolion yn ymwybodol o'u diwylliant cynhenid.

Fel y rhan fwyaf o drefi Cymru a Lloegr mae Stryd Fawr Yr Wyddgrug wedi colli peth o'i statws oherwydd i ormod o siopau gwerthu tai ac elusennau gymryd trosodd unedau gwâg, tra bo archfarchnadoedd yn disodli'r siopau bach. Serch hynny, mae'r hen draddodiad o farchnad agored yn gwerthu nwyddau ac anifeiliaid yn ffynnu'n wythnosol, ar ddyddiau Mercher a Sadwrn. Yn wir, yn 2006 gwelwyd am y tro cyntaf, gynnyrch yr ardal yn cael ei glodfori mewn G yl Bwyd a Diod a gynhaliwyd dan nawdd Marchnad Ffermwyr Yr Wyddgrug.

Mae yna ddigon i'w weld a gwneud yma. Bydd pob math o chwaraeon i'w gwylio neu gymryd rhan ynddynt, a llu o dai bwyta i'ch bodloni. Yn y Llyfrgell mae amgueddfa lle gellir gweld copi o'r clogyn aur a ffeithiau diddorol yngl n â'r dref ar ardal gyfagos. Yno hefyd ceir gwybodaeth am enwogion lleol, yn eu mysg yr arlunydd Richard Wilson (1713–1782), y cerddor John Ambrose Lloyd (1815–1874) ar nofelydd Daniel Owen (1836–1895).

Bydd Cymdeithas Ddinesig Yr Wyddgrug a'r Cylch yn cynnal darlithoedd drwy gydol y flwyddyn a chyhoeddi cylchgrawn hanes: *Ystrad Alun*. Yn ddiweddar, cynhyrchwyd CD-ROM o'r ardal gyda 1600 o ddelweddau arni. Hefyd, o bryd i'w gilydd, codir plac yma ac acw yn y cyffiniau i gofio person neu ddigwyddiad arbennig.

Ceir gwybodaeth am y Gymdeithas gan david@daverowe.co.uk neu gan Mrs Diane Johnson ar typedwar@tiscali.co.uk

Rwyn gobeithio y gwnewch fwynhau fy siwrnai fer. Mae cymaint o agweddau eraill nad oedd modd eu crybwyll mewn llyfr fel hwn lle mae'r pwyslais ar luniau. Os ydych yn byw yn lleol, gobeithio wir y dysgwch rywbeth newydd am eich bro. Os dieithryn ydych, peidiwch â'i gadael yn rhy hwyr cyn ymweld â ni!

David Rowe

SOME THOUGHTS ON MOLD

For although unbearable sorrow had invaded the prince's mind, yet through the providence of God unexpected joy raised him up. For there was a certain castle called Mold which had frequently been besieged without success. And when Owain's courtiers and war-band came to lay siege to it, neither the nature of the place nor its strength could resist them till the castle was burnt and till it was ravaged, after some of the garrison had been slain and others had been captured and imprisoned.

(English translation of *Brut Y Tywysogyon* / *The Chronicle of the Princes*, 1146)

Were I to curse the man I hate
From youth till I grow old
Oh! Might he be condemned by fate
To waste his days in Mold

(Richard Brinsley Sheridan, 1751–1816)

Pretty Mold
Proud People
Handsome Church
Without Steeple

(Anon, late 1700s. The steeple was added in 1768.)

In our way to this place we stopt for refreshment at Mold, where we examined the Church, and observed a monument erected by some foolish fellow to *himself* professing his dislike of flattery. The Country we passed through is of particular beauty.

(Dr Samuel Johnson, *A Journey into North Wales in the Year 1774*)

While there are cliffs in Snowdonia
While there are trees on Bailey Hill
While there is water in the river Alun
I'll keep a pure heart for SOMEONE

(Revd John Blackwell, Bardic name Alun, 1797-1840)

It is a small market town, consisting principally of one long and wide street. The church is a neat building ornamented all round the top of the outside walls with gothic carvings of animals. The body was erected in the reign of Henry VII but the tower is of more modern date.

(Revd W. Bingley, *North Wales*, 1814)

'Few towns have altered more in their character during the past 40 years than that of Mold. At the commencement of that period, it was a quiet country place, only enlivened on market and fair days and at assize time, and holding little communication with the surrounding places of larger traffic; its public conveyance being confined to the carriers' wagon twice a week to Chester ... Of its picturesqueness and beauty, stranger tourists, visiting the place, generally express their admiration.

(C.H. Leslie, *Rambles around Mold*, 1869)

The jaded sojourner in crowded cities in quest of rejuvenation and quietude "Far from the madding crowd" might with advantage direct his attention to the natural charms and health restoring properties of pretty MOLD.

(From a council guidebook from the 1920s)

...serious drama and dance at Theatr Clwyd in Mold – though beware the foyer, with its full-frontal panorama of the hills. You might never make it into the auditorium.

(Vincent Crump, *Sunday Times*, 21 January 2007)

1

Historic Events

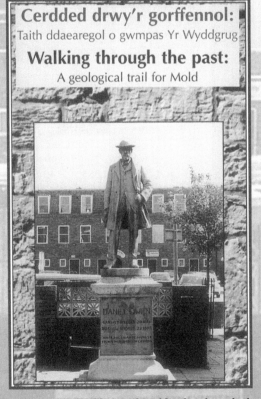

Cerdded drwy'r gorffennol:
Taith ddaearegol o gwmpas Yr Wyddgrug

Walking through the past:
A geological trail for Mold

Most of the stone used in the earlier buildings of Mold is local, with the majority comprised of sandstone with roofs made from either local slate or imported from Blaenau Ffestiniog. The oldest material would appear to be the pebbles outside DSG Chartered Accountants in Grosvenor Street, dating from the Triassic period some 250 million years ago. The walking trail leaflet is available from the town library.

Above: Ranked as one of the top ten treasures of the British Museum, the Mold Gold Cape has been restored to its full glory. Discovered in a burial mound in Chester Road during road works in 1833 (a plaque in the wall marks the spot), the piece is quite unique. Made from a single ingot of gold, it probably had a backing of leather or cloth and is likely to have been used for ceremonial purposes, although its exact use is not known. A replica of the cape can be found in the small museum located in the town library. *(Paul Davies)*

Left: Just outside Mold, on the Rhual Estate, is a field called Maes Garmon, which is considered to have been the site of a battle in AD 447 between the Christian Britons, led by Bishop Germanus of Auxerre, and a pagan force comprising Picts and Scots. With the armies facing each other, the Britons are reputed to have cried out 'Alleluia, Alleluia', thereby making the pagans believe the Christian force was larger than it really was. As a result, they fled and reports say they were either killed or drowned in the nearby River Alyn. *(Eric Keen)*

Right: Mold does not appear in the Domesday Book (1086), although nearby townships such as Gwysaney and Bistre do, but the Normans left their mark with the motte and bailey castle on what we now know as Bailey Hill. The original Norman family responsible for erecting the castle were the Montalts (Mohaut) and this may be the source of the town's English name, Mold. The castle was believed to be only a wooden structure and information is limited, but hopefully more details will be unearthed if funds can be found to carry out a full archaeological dig. *(Ken Lloyd Gruffydd)*

Mohaut / Castell Yr Wyddgrug, c.1210.

Below: Ken Lloyd Gruffydd attributes the first stone-built church to Radalph de Mohaut (1162–1199) and it is believed that these stone carvings were part of the original church. These, along with other corbels, have been incorporated into wall capping opposite the old cottage hospital in Pwll Glas. *(Eric Keen)*

Left: The first record of a church is in the Norwich Taxation of 1253, but the present much-altered St Mary's Church dates from around 1485. Following the victory of her son Henry Tudor at the battle of Bosworth, Margaret Beaufort, wife of Sir Thomas Stanley, sponsored the building of the church as a celebration of his victory over Richard III. Further churches were also built at Gresford, Hope and Northop, along with St Winifrede's Chapel at Holywell. All of these churches contain Stanley family heraldry. *(Eric Keen)*

Below: The first reference to Gwysaney occurs in the Domesday Book, but the present house dates from around 1603. There has been a considerable amount of subsequent renovation and re-building. On 3 April 1645, Sir William Brereton led Parliamentarian troops to Mold and attacked Gwysaney, then the home of the Royalist Lt-Col. Thomas Davies, where it is recorded they took twenty-seven prisoners. The holes left by musket balls can still be found in the front door. *(Eric Keen)*

Above: Plas Teg (Fair Mansion) has a reputation as the most haunted house in Wales and poses a challenge to many societies and groups dedicated to the investigation of the paranormal. Built in 1608 for Sir John Trevor, he became secretary to Lord Howard of Effingham and exploited his share of lucrative positions to the full. The house is unique in Wales, and while it has faced dilapidation and demolition on more than one occasion, the house and gardens have been privately restored and are open to the public on Sunday afternoons. *(Eric Keen)*

Right: The current owner of Plas Teg, Mrs Cornelia Bayley, is responsible for the continuing restoration work of the house and gardens, and without her dedication and considerable expenditure, it is likely the house would have become a total ruin. The extensive restoration includes the provision of statues throughout the grounds and the example shown adds further character to the surroundings. *(Eric Keen)*

Court House

Parish Church

Railway Bridge
on Chester Street

Railway
Inn

1st House is where
Blackwell was born

This rare photograph was taken in 1870, one year after the Mold Riots, and two of the key buildings involved in the tragedy can be seen; the courthouse (above the railway bridge) and the railway station. Following ongoing disputes between the local miners and the English manager at Leeswood Green colliery, the miners ran the manager out of town setting off a fatal chain of events. Following the trial, a number of miners were taken to the railway station for transportation to Flint Gaol where a large crowd stoned the troops and the police guarding them. Eventually the troops opened fire, killing four people. *(Flintshire Record Office, 40/162)*

2

High Street

This early image of Mold in quieter times will still be recognisable to today's visitor, as the view remains dominated by St Mary's Church. The tall building in the foreground is the townhouse of George Wynne of Leeswood Hall, who we will meet later. To the right of the house is a workshop where Daniel Owen, considered by many to be the Welsh equivalent of Charles Dickens, trained as a tailor, and to the left is the Black Lion Hotel. *(Ray Davies)*

This rare photograph, taken around the 1860s, shows the Cross and is comprised of a fountain and clock. Erected in 1864 to commemorate the death of Prince Albert, it stood on a raised base and beneath the clock hung medallions. The fountain was finally removed in 1884 as it was considered a traffic hazard and 'a resort for idlers'. The clock was subsequently mounted on the outside of the Assembly Hall. *(Flintshire Record Office)*

Taken from the balcony of the Assembly Hall, this photograph shows one of the many parades that took place in the High Street, with the Star Hotel in the foreground and the County Supply Stores to the left. The canopy of the County Stores was erected in 1899 and therefore provides a datum point for dating photographs. *(Glynn Morris)*

Following the end of the Boer War in 1902, trees were planted in the High Street to commemorate the event, and this photograph shows the young trees. The condition of the relatively deserted street at this time looks quite good but this was not always the case. In 1887 the *Wrexham Advertiser*, responding to complaints from residents, visited the High Street and concluded that 'with the aid of a few stepping stones and a good boat, together with the exercise of ordinary caution and perseverance, a skilled person might cross the street with comparative safety.' *(Ray Davies)*

High Street, Mold.

Following the death on 1 July 1913 of PC James Blythen while on traffic control duty at the junction of the High Street, King Street and Earl Road during the Annual Diocesan festival of the Mothers Union, Mold Urban District Council sought to procure a speed limit of 5mph as there was great concern over the steady increase of motor traffic. *(Ray Davies)*

Electric street lighting was introduced to the town in 1927 and a light standard can be observed on the left of this picture. A bus can be seen heading up the road, along with what are still a limited number of motor vehicles. Glazier's shop on the right-hand side of the street was a well-known store that, following their move to Wrexham Street, operated the first travel agency in Mold. *(Ray Davies)*

One of the first of a chain of Iceland shops that spread across the UK, the company has become a major player in the retail trade as well as a major employer at its Deeside Industrial Park headquarters. Sadly, the pressure of modern commerce's need to cut costs has seen much of the operation being moved out of the area with resulting job losses. *(Glynn Morris)*

In 1928, nineteen grocers and tea dealers were listed as operating in the four main
streets, a figure that has now fallen to zero, although the town maintains three main
supermarkets; Tesco, Aldi and Somerfield. To the right of Tesco and next to the Midland
Bank is the Cambrian public house. This has since been demolished and is now a
passageway to the precinct and indoor market. *(Glynn Morris)*

Mold Town Council provides the Christmas lights each year and the switching-on
ceremony sees the lower part of the High Street closed to accommodate the fair and
other attractions. As can be seen from this 1998 photograph, they provide an attractive
scene encouraging people from outside the area to shop in Mold. *(Eric Keen)*

Various efforts have been made to make the lower part of the High Street more
pedestrian friendly including, in 1995, the decorative paving of the lower High Street.
The picture also shows three shops; Freeman Hardy Willis, Greenwoods and Fosters,
which have all now disappeared from the High Street to be replaced by Shoefayre,
an unnamed kitchen accessory shop and Specsavers. The make up of the businesses
operating in the town centre has changed over the decades, as the following selection of
businesses listed in the 1835 Pigot Trade Directory demonstrates:

Academies & Schools	9
Blacksmiths and Farriers	7
Boot and Shoemakers	8
Butchers	13
Coopers	2
Corn Merchants	3
Curriers	3
Grocers	13
Joiners	3
Linen and Woollen Drapers	9
Malsters	10
Milliners and Dressmakers	5
Mining Companies	16
Saddlers	5
Inns, Taverns and Public Houses	22
Retailers of Beer	18
Tailors	10
Wheelwrights	3

(Eric Keen)

This 1996 photograph shows a jazz band launching the opening of the relatively short-lived Energy Centre. With competition from out of town shopping, it must be very difficult for specialist traders to remain profitable in what is, after all, a limited catchment area. *(Eric Keen)*

This part of the High Street has changed dramatically with the majority of the buildings on the left-hand side having been demolished in the 1950s, and Cilcen (Cilcain) Road now renamed Pwll Glas. *(Eric Keen)*

This 1950 photograph of the upper High Street shows three of the shops that were demolished in order to open up the front of St Mary's Church and includes two well-known family names in Mold; Brannan's and the watchmaker and jeweller, C.W. Kunstle. Among the other clock and watchmakers operating in the High Street was Severin Lehmann (1860–1883) who was a native of Baden, Germany, and whose assistant was Joseph Saum. *(Glynn Morris)*

Contemporary records show the business with the names Saum and Lehmann, and
following the death of Lehmann, the business continued to be run by Joseph Saum, as
can be seen from this early postcard. *(Ray Davies)*

These three buildings pictured in 1979 still exist and W. Thomas's shoe shop is
still operating and run by the octogenarian Mrs Thomas and her son Graham. Ron
Hammersley, a well-known character, continues to run his business on the opposite side
of the High Street. J.H. Jones and Discount Pet Food Centre now occupy the other two
buildings and a new building exists on the right of Thomas's shoe shop. *(Glynn Morris)*

3

Churches & Chapels

Located in Glanrafon Road, the Bethabara Baptist Church ceased to be a chapel in the 1880s and has since had a variety of uses including being used as a warehouse by well-known local oil merchant and chandler, Fred Dyment. It is now used as a chapel of rest for local undertakers James Hughes & Sons. In the background of this 2003 photograph, the English Wesleyan Methodist Chapel in Wrexham Street can be seen. *(Ray Davies)*

EBENEZER

BAPTIST CHURCH

WREXHAM STREET
MOLD

1880 CENTENARY 1980

Left: The Ebenezer Baptist Church was opened on Easter Sunday 1880 at a cost of £860 and was replaced in the 1980s by the new church in Glanrafon. The building now houses an electrical wholesaler and fireplace shop. The building of the church was funded by public subscription and when money ran out, Rhiannon Griffiths' great-grandmother, Elizabeth Griffiths, assisted by selling a cow for around £8, thereby allowing building work to continue. A 1905 report into Nonconformist churches described it as Welsh Baptist with 210 'adherents'. *(Rhiannon Griffiths)*

Below: The Welsh Church Commission 'County of Flint – Statistics of the Nonconformist Churches for 1905' describes the chapel as the Pentre Calvinistic Methodist. Built in 1853 under the umbrella of the Bethesda Chapel, the building was located on Chester Road, finally being demolished in the 1980s. No new building has taken place on the site. *(Ray Davies)*

Right: Built in the 1890s, the English Presbyterian Church was demolished in 1973 with the stone being re-used at Chester Zoo, and the K. Hugh Dodd auction rooms now occupy the site. The chapel is one of the many buildings that have disappeared or are no longer used for religious purposes. How different then from the description of Welsh Nonconformist chapels by Sir Thomas Philips in 1849: 'reared up by the poor dwellers of the mountain valleys, in every corner in which a few Christian men are congregated, and these buildings are thronged by earnest minded worshippers assembled for religious services...' *(Ray Davies)*

Below: From the 1795 St Asaph Diocesan records, it is believed that the first Nonconformist chapel was housed in a 'Room or Building together with a Dwelling House' at Ponterwyl, and the location is now marked by a plaque. The current Calvinistic Methodist Bethesda Chapel was rebuilt in 1863 by W.W. Gwyther of London but has a previous inscription of 1819. Daniel Owen attended the chapel and it is where the Revd Roger Edwards nurtured Daniel's literary talents. *(Glynn Morris)*

Above: This photograph was taken from the top of St Mary's Church and shows the listed Pendref Welsh Wesleyan Chapel (now known as the King's Church) and the summit of the motte on Bailey Hill. The chapel was opened on 6 July 1828 when Revd Thomas preached to a large congregation, with another 2,000 gathered on Bailey Hill. Sir Thomas Mostyn donated the land for the chapel and the heavily patterned stone is believed to have come from one of his quarries. *(Ray Davies)*

Left: As detailed in Chapter 1, the first church was recorded in 1253 but Margaret Beaufort was responsible for the building of a new church in 1485. Over the years, the church has undergone many changes, including restoration and enlargement by Sir Gilbert Scott in 1856. The church contains many memorial tablets commemorating the prominent families who were among the church's benefactors. A number of informative publications detailing the history of the church are available. *(Ray Davies)*

Above: Following the demolition of the shops and houses in the 1950s and the removal of many of the gravestones and memorials, the area at the front of the church was landscaped and the retaining wall built. The stone used for the wall was reclaimed from the Bethel Chapel at Llong – which was demolished in 1954 – and includes the name stone for the chapel. Unfortunately, this was placed inwards and all efforts to identify its location have failed. *(Glynn Morris)*

Right: The original peal of six bells by Rudhall of Gloucester date from about 1732 and this photograph shows them being removed for transportation to Loughborough in October 2005. The original bells were refurbished and along with two newly cast bells, have been reinstalled. Apart from the pealing of bells for services these can also be heard on Tuesday evenings when the bell-ringing practices are held. *(Eric Keen)*

Above: The earliest reference to a church at Nercwys – regarded as one of the ancient parishes of Flintshire – is 1291, but is described as a 'chapelry of the parish of Mold'. Extensively restored and enlarged in 1847 and again in 1882–3, at a cost of £2,100, the church remains a place of worship today. The church pictured in the early 1900s has undergone many alterations and repairs. The fine example of woodcarving to the right of the altar is worthy of closer examination. *(Ray Davies)*

Left: This 2001 photograph of St Mary's, Nercwys, belies the concerns expressed in a 1640 complaint about 'spiritual destitution and clerical neglect' and the abuse of the Sabbath. 'Most of the youths and yonger sorte of people in either parishe doe commonoly haunt the hare with greyhounds and houndes upon the Sundayes in the morninge, or doe use to play the foot boole ... the elder sorte doe commonly fall to drinking or some unlawfull games.' *(Eric Keen)*

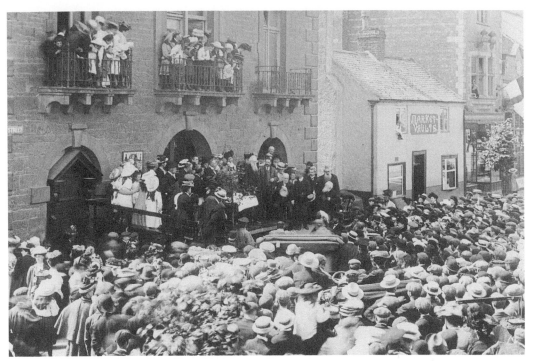

General Booth, the founder of the Salvation Army, visited Mold in 1906 and, as can be seen in this photograph, attracted large crowds whenever he appeared. While this initial meeting was held outside the Assembly Hall, the Salvation Army now has premises in Wrexham Street. The area already had a long tradition of nonconformity and a survey of church attendances in 1851 gave the following figures:

Anglican	22%	Calvinistic Methodist	24%
Independent	12%	Other	7%
Baptist	6%	Unrecorded	8%
Wesleyan Methodist	21%	(Ray Davies)	

Right: The first recorded Catholic church was erected in 1862 and built by parishioners, despite the abuse and occasional violence shown to them by townspeople. This photograph shows old and new together in 1966 when Bishop John Petit consecrated the new church, which cost £45,000 to build. The adjacent La Sainte Union Convent was completed in 1963 and a number of the Sisters taught at St David's Catholic School. *(George Tattum)*

TOC H MOLD

Souvenir Brochure
a n d
Service of Dedication
o f
Cathrina House

SATURDAY, 13th JULY, 1968

at 3 p.m.

TOC H had been operating in Mold since 1932 but the purpose-built Cathrina House was opened on 13 July 1968. The building is now a children's nursery. The organisation was founded in 1915 when Army Padre 'Tubby' Clayton established a rest centre in Flanders called Talbot House and used as its symbol a cross surmounting a Roman lamp. In 1922 the organisation received a Royal Charter and local branches were operating in Buckley, Ruthin, Queensferry, Flint, Hope and Caergwrle and Llanarmon yn Ial.

Commerce

General Coach Smiths,

For researchers, trade directories of this nature are invaluable as they offer a snapshot of life within a town or area. As can be seen from the 1886 directory, thirty-six grocers were operating within Mold. Just three stores have replaced the small businesses and none of the four listed hotels remain in business. The Star and Royal Oak buildings no longer exist, the Victoria is now a dental surgery and the remaining portion of the Black Lion is a building society.

SPECIAL OFFER

(FOR A FEW DAYS ONLY) AT

Tea HUNTERS' Stores

LEAN BREAKFAST BACON

Sliced **9½** D. Per lb.

TENDER BOILED HAM

PER **5** D. QTR.

BUMPER PARCEL

OF

Seasonable Goods

	USUAL PRICE
1 Tin BAKED BEANS -	3½d.
1¼-lb. Pkt. PURE COCOA	2½d.
1 lb. EMPIRE RICE - -	2d.
1 lb. PORAGE OATS -	1¾d.
1 lb. GREEN PEAS - -	2¼d.
1 Large Pkt. SALT - -	1d.

—FOR—

10 D.   ~~1/1~~

THE LOT

AND YOU'LL NEED THEM ALL!

FULL-CREAM CHESHIRE CHEESE

PER **6** D. LB.

WHOLESOME BISCUITS

GINGER SNAPS - - BEST BUTTER - - THIN LUNCH, ETC. } **5½** d. PER LB.

ASSORTED CREAMS } From **6** d.

CEREALS are CHEAPER—OURS are also THE BEST !

	PER LB.			PER LB.
New Loose OATS - - } OATMEAL (All Grades) }	**1½** d.	Rangoon BEANS - - } Pearl BARLEY - - }	**1¼** d.	
Empire RICE - - } BUTTER BEANS - }	**2** d.	**PEAS**: Marrowfats - 3d. Good Green - 2¼d.		
MACARONI—½-lb. Box }	**2½** d.	TAPIOCAS—Seed or Medium **2½** d.		

A FEW MORE BARGAINS TAKEN AT RANDOM :

BAKED BEANS, Large Tin, 3½d. — CORNED BEEF, Sliced, 6d. lb. — ONIONS, 1½d. lb.
GOOD APPLES, Eat or Bake - 2½d. lb.——STRAWBERRY JAM, Large Jar - 7½d.
LARGE TIN PINEAPPLE - 5½d.—GIANT PACKET OF PEAS - 2½d. — Etc., Etc.

HUNTERS for BEST VALUE!

An advertisement for Hunters Stores in Chester Street, Mold, now a solicitor's office. It is interesting to compare these prices with those of our modern supermarkets. *(Anne Woodward)*

Taken in February 1925, this photograph shows five-year-old Jennie Foulkes (*née* Sandall) with her father and their horse-drawn High Class Fish and Chip cart. Mr Sandall incurred the wrath of Mold Urban District Council who criticised him for setting up in the wrong place at night. In summer the chip fryer was replaced with equipment for making ice cream. A wonderful lady, Jennie passed away in 2007 but her memory will live on with all who had the privilege to know her. (*Mrs Jennie Foulkes*)

The building on the corner is the Britannia Inn, still operating in 2007. Although fashion and the lack of traffic in this 1908 photo have changed somewhat, the view remains recognisable to today's shoppers. Many of the buildings remain, albeit with altered frontages, and in the case of the Assembly Hall, the third floor has been removed. The block on the left currently includes Hulson's shop, and a testament to the popularity and quality of its products can be seen from the queues that form outside on Saturdays. (*Ray Davies*)

Left: Taken in about 1947, this photograph shows Mrs Elsie Kendrick dispensing milk for a young Rhiannon Griffiths. In today's world, such a method of retailing milk would be considered unhygienic and therefore would not be allowed. The Kendricks were a well-known family in and around Mold and lived at the Park, which is now all housing, while the old dairy on New Street is now an agricultural merchant's store. *(Rhiannon Griffiths)*

Below: In 1920 John Griffiths bought nos 35–7 Wrexham Street to carry on his butchery business, and on his death in 1936, two of his sons, William and Llewelyn, ran the business together. In 1952 William branched out on his own with a shop in Chester Street while Llewelyn continued in Wrexham Street until 1967 when he sold the business to Gwilym Williams. The property now houses Hulson's shop. *(Rhiannon Griffiths)*

Above and right: This letterhead and 1921 postcard bring together two of the major contributors of photographs for this journey: Rhiannon Griffiths's grandfather, John Griffiths, and Ray Davies' uncle, J.D. Jones. A sign of the times when you could send a postcard to your local butcher – but note that John may not have been too pleased as the card was under-stamped and excess postage of 1d was payable. *(Rhiannon Griffiths)*

37, WREXHAM STREET,
MOLD,

_____ 19___

M _____

Bought of

JOHN GRIFFITHS
Family Butcher,

Home-Made Sausages.   :   Pressed Beef.
Home-Cured Bacon and Hams.   :   Brawn & Black Puddings

DAILY DELIVERIES, PROMPT PERSONAL ATTENTION

Photographed here in the 1950s, the Mold Savings Bank (now a charity shop) is located on the corner of High Street and Earl Road. The railings have long gone as, I suspect, has the car disappearing down Earl Road. Prior to the building of Earl Road, the bank was the site of the carriage turning circle for visitors to the original Keene and Kelly office located directly behind. *(Rhiannon Griffiths)*

The staff shown in this 1950 photograph are Miss Eileen Rowlands, the manageress on the left, assistant Miss Hilda Probert on the right and an unknown lady on the far right. The ledgers, all completed by hand, are a far cry from the modern computerised systems currently in use in Mold's many banks and building societies. The need for security screens had not been found to be necessary at that time. *(Rhiannon Griffiths)*

Just visible above the sign for the Armon Dining Room is the roof of the Bethesda Chapel, which enables today's visitor to put the buildings in their correct locations. The shop in the right foreground of this early 1900s photograph is now a pet shop, next door is a ladies' hairdressers with the entrance into the one of the town's car park adjoining. *(Ray Davies)*

The scene in 1984 changes as we move further down New Street with the sign for Y Pentan in the centre of the picture, including the building that originally housed Daniel Owen's tailor's shop. A memorial plaque on the side of the building commemorates the link. The name of the public house is derived from an 1895 Daniel Owen novel entitled *Straeon y Pentan / Fireside Stories*. *(Glynn Morris)*

This 1984 photograph was taken from outside Bargain Wallpapers and shows the indoor
market in the centre and the New Street car park. The indoor market has been relocated
and the car park has disappeared under a new block of shops with offices on the first floor.
Stanton's has been replaced by a video shop and, due to the removal of parking spaces, other
businesses have come and gone. *(Glynn Morris)*

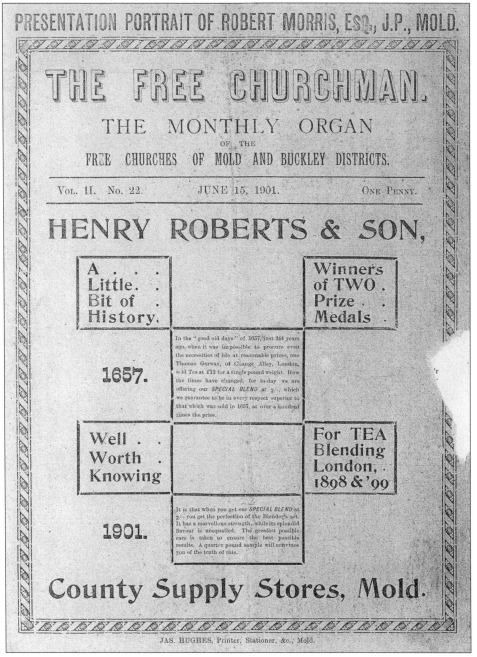

One of the useful sources for historical research is advertisements in newspapers or other publications. This County Supply Stores advertisement is taken from a publication called the *Free Churchman*. Published monthly, it was the official journal of the Free Churches of Mold and Buckley districts and is likely to have had a large circulation, thereby making it an attractive proposition for businesses. The County Supply Stores was located in Mold High Street and could be identified by the canopy across the pavement. (*Rhiannon Griffiths*)

The second extract from the *Free Churchman* contains three advertisements, two of which have further stories to tell. Henry Lloyd Jones, a Liberal, served as an Alderman and was respected throughout the area, but tragedy struck when some of his workers died, possibly from TB. Compton House still exists but was rebuilt in 1929. Does anyone know what prompted the statement regarding American beef in the Pugh advertisement? *(Rhiannon Griffiths)*

Above: Agriculture has always been a major industry in the area but it has not always been peaceful, as during the Tithe Wars of 1886–91, farmers led the way in the disputes with the Anglican Church on the question of the payment of tithes. These protests were spurred on by an upsurge in Welsh Liberalism and the dislike of the mainly nonconformist tenants over-paying tithes to what was seen as a foreign church and rents to absentee English Tory landlords. *(Eric Keen)*

Right: This example of a 1926 Tithe Rent charge to the Welsh Church Commission records the enactment of a new Act in 1891. *(Ann Woodward)*

Despite the recent challenges posed by foot and mouth disease and general problems associated with agriculture, the farmer's market has survived and continues to attract farmers from throughout the area. Sheep continue to be a major feature on the hills, and between January and April, lambs provide a wonderful pastoral scene. However, this image belies the difficulties and hardships many farmers are faced with in trying to earn a decent living. *(Eric Keen)*

One of the pleasures of being involved in a project of this nature is the variety of people you meet, one such person being Mrs Maenwen Williams whose late husband, George, farmed at Cefn Melyn, Cilcain. In 1983 George and his dog Don won the Welsh National Sheepdog trials. This photograph shows a number of trophies he won, including the rose bowl engraved with the words 'Langs Supreme Welsh Champion 1983'. *(Ray Davies)*

Among the traditional pursuits held within the agricultural community are ploughing competitions and in this photograph we see a mode of power used in earlier times. The competition was held in a field adjoining the Denbigh road and the beautiful Shire horse can be seen ploughing its furrow in competition with the more traditional tractors. *(Eric Croall)*

Cheese making appears in a number of locations and this photograph shows trainees at a cheese making class held at Nercwys Hall, although whether they were to be employed by the Nerquis and District Co-operative Cheese-Making Society Ltd remains unclear. The Co-operative was registered in 1918 under the Industrial and Provident Societies Act and was housed in a former colliery building that exists today as a private house. *(Ray Davies)*

The old bakery of the North Wales Cake Co. was located at what is now the Bryn Awel Hotel and, from the number of medals and awards it received, it was clearly producing high quality products. Like the Glanrafon Bakery, which closed in June 2006, many of the independents have either been swallowed up by large concerns or have found continuing production uneconomical. *(Ray Davies)*

A date stone found in this building in King Street gives a date of 1776 and since then, the building has seen a variety of uses, although many of the older residents will remember it as the Beehive. In 2006 the shop was transformed from Spaven's newsagent into an ice-cream parlour and 'sweetie heaven' selling many old and new favourites. A popular haunt, it is nice to see a business reinvent itself to meet new challenges. *(Eric Keen)*

5

Hotels & Pubs

When I first moved to Mold, without my family, I lived in the Bryn Awel Hotel and met, among other people, one of the major contributor's to this book, Ray Davies, and little did we know that fifteen or so years later we would become friends and collaborate on a number of projects. Our first joint research twenty-three years ago was to carry out 'field trips' to the local hostelries, many of which have now ceased trading. Over the years, around fifty public houses/hotels have operated in Mold and the following listing may trigger a few memories.

Alyn Temperance Hotel
Black Boy
Black Horse
Black Lion Hotel
Blue Bell
Boars Head*
Bowling Green Hotel
Bridge Inn*
Britannia Inn
Brown Cow
Bryn Awel Hotel*
Bryn Griffith (Top) Club*
Butchers Arms
Carriages
Cambrian
Chester Arms
Colliers Arms
Conservative Club
Corbett's Vaults
Corkers Wine Bar*
Cross Keys (Y Pentan)
Crown Vaults
Dolphin Hotel*
Dragon

Drovers Arms*
Ex-Serviceman's Club*
Feathers Inn
Flounders or Founders
Glasfryn*
Gold Cape*
Golden Lion
Griffin Inn*
Gwysaney Arms
Hare and Hounds
Hawaden Castle
Henry Letts or Crown Vaults
Kings Head
Leeswood Arms
Liverpool Arms
Lord Hill
Mason's Arms
Market Vaults
Milkhouse
Miner's Arms
Old Vaults
Pickled Herring
Pied Bull - Pentre
Queens Head*

Railway Inn (Carriages)
Rainbow
Raven
Red Lion*
Roebuck
Ropers Arms
Royal Oak – New Street
Royal Oak – Gwysaney
Royal Oak – Rhyd y Goleu
Ruthin Castle*
Sameplace
Star Hotel
Sun Inn
Swan-Pentre
Talbot
Tafarn Derwen Inn
The Grosvenor Hotel
The Mostyn Arms
Travellers Rest – Pentre
Union
Upper Vaults
Vaults
Victoria Hotel
White Horse
White Lion

*Still operating at the time of writing.

Left: Listed in an 1876 trade directory, the Brown Cow was located at 82 High Street and this photograph shows the then landlord, Thomas Jones. The large number of pubs may be the result of the influx of miners and the need to cater for their needs. Certainly many of the outlying villages had a number of public houses that was disproportionate to local population numbers. *(Ray Davies)*

Below: In 1835 the Black Lion was described as an inn with a posting house and among the staff listed in the 1881 census was a boy billiard marker. During the Second World War British Intelligence misled the Germans into believing that the initial invasion of southern Europe was not to be through Sicily. As part of this deception they created the character of a Major Martin whose body was washed up on a Spanish beach. Among the papers in his briefcase were two letters from his 'father' written on Black Lion notepaper and these contributed towards successfully convincing the Germans to move troops out of Sicily. *(Ray Davies)*

Beloved of real ale aficionados, this small traditional public house, the Colomendy Arms, has had the same landlord for almost twenty years and attracts visitors from all over the country. Situated in the small village of Cadole, it is adjacent to the extensive lead mines that operated in the area in previous centuries. The village had previously been called Cathole, and a theory has been expounded that it was given the name by the many Cornish miners working the area to differentiate it from Mousehole in Cornwall. *(Ray Davies)*

The present timber frame structure of the Dolphin Hotel as viewed in 1993 was built at the turn of the twentieth century and replaced a much older timber frame public house. The 1835 edition of the Pigot trade directory records that the inn also housed the Excise Office, which is confirmed in the 1876 edition with a John Moore as supervisor. A subscription bowling club also operated from the back of the premises for many years. *(Eric Keen)*

Situated on the corner of the High Street and Chester Street, the Grosvenor Hotel is now the premises of an estate agent. To the right of this 1920s picture is the Henry Lloyd Jones Compton House shop. Note the total lack of traffic and the finger direction post mounted on the lamppost. During the early 1900s a Colonel Platt of Bangor owned the hotel and the licensee was named as Alfred Davies. *(Ray Davies)*

Built in 1931 to a design by the leading architect Sir Clough Williams-Ellis (of Portmeirion fame), this was the first purpose-built hostel by a prominent architect. Located in 5½ acres outside Maeshafn, the wooden single-storey building was comprised of one room with four beds, one with six, one with nine and one with twelve. However, tastes have changed and due to lack of visitors, it closed in 2004 and the grade II listed building is now a Relaxation and Holistic Therapy Centre. *(Ray Davies)*

This was not the original Market Vaults building on this site, and it ceased trading as a public house in the 1990s. A clothes shop now carries out its business in the premises. The ground floor has completely changed from this 1986 view, with large windows now displaying the shop's wares. The right-hand window advertises the fact that this was a smoke room, but following the Welsh Assembly government legislation effective 2 April 2007, which banned smoking in public buildings, smokers now have to go outside. *(Eric Keen)*

Pigot's trade directory of 1835 lists Hugh Jones as the landlord of the Masons Arms, located at the top of the High Street, and this photograph shows a charabanc trip outside, the landlord at this time being William T. Mitchell. To the right of the main building are three smaller buildings, the two on the right have since been demolished but it is still possible to identify the buildings that are now private houses. *(Ray Davies)*

The Mostyn Arms stood at 56 Milford Street in the area known as Bedlam and was the meeting place of Daniel Owen and his literary group, a factor that led to concerted effort to prevent its demolition. Seen here in 1984, the building had seen better days and was finally demolished shortly afterwards. In the 1840s, Milford Street ran from the High Street through to the Bridge Inn and contained a number of boarding houses and public houses and it is this area where many of the Irish community lived. *(Ray Davies)*

The Owain Glyndwr Hotel is located on the edge of the village of Gwernymynydd and holds an annual festival to commemorate the man considered by many Welsh people to be the last true Prince of Wales, Owain Glyndwr (*c*.1353–*c*.1416). In 1400, following extreme provocation, Owain rebelled and over the following years conquered most of Wales until, in 1415 following military reversals, he simply disappeared. In Shakespeare's *Henry IV, Part I*, Glyndwr is mentioned in several places, being described in one as 'a worthy gentlemen, exceeding well read'. *(Ray Davies)*

Originally a single storey dwelling, the Ruthin Castle has incorporated a number of adjoining cottages and is now recognised as a traditional town pub where the landlord expects his customers to conform to acceptable levels of behaviour. Those who choose not to will not be served! In 1920, Price's field was opposite and in the Mold Urban District Council minutes of that year, mention is made of a nuisance caused by traction engines and a WC. The decision was taken to screen the WC! *(Ray Davies)*

Located towards the lower end of the High Street, the Star Hotel has now been demolished but during its lifetime the building was one of the four hotels in Mold and evidence of its livery stable can still be seen today. Although faded, the livery building sign is still visible on the side of the building at the High Street entrance to the cattle market. The Star also had its own brewery during its operating days. On the corner, the Grosvenor Hotel can be seen. *(Ray Davies)*

Above: In 1868 The Tafarn Derwen (The Oak) was an isolated inn surrounded by fields but within easy reach of the nearby Broncoed and Oak Pit collieries. The landlord at the time, Patrick Kinnair, justified the renewal of his licence by stating that the collieries needed to buy brandy from him to deal with medical emergencies. The building ceased operation as a public house two years ago and currently stands empty and awaiting redevelopment. *(Ray Davies)*

Left: October 2006 saw the inauguration of an annual food fair held in the town car park next to Somerfield supermarket. This was part of a campaign to highlight the wide range of produce available in Mold and surrounding areas. With an estimated three and a half million people living within a thirty-minute drive from Mold, the opportunities for food purveyors are extremely high. The 2007 fair was well attended and it is hoped that attendances will increase year on year.

6

Houses

One resident of the now demolished Bromfield Hall was David Williams, co-founder of the Alyn Tin Plate Works (*see* Chapter 7), but most people will associate the hall with Peter Roberts. Roberts made his fortune through the production of rotateable rubber soles on shoes and pneumatic tyres, and he can be seen to the right of the doorway. A generous benefactor, he donated the Town Hall to the town. Local legend claims that the staircase, now at Portmeirion, is the same one Lady Jane Grey walked down prior to her execution.

(Ray Davies)

Mold had a number of coalmines and these attracted workers from all corners of the UK and housing was required to accommodate the workers and their families. The houses in Bromfield Row, demolished in 1971, were located near the Bromfield colliery and are typical examples of the type of terraced houses available and would have had very limited facilities. *(Ray Davies)*

Situated on the edge of the village of Rhydymwyn, Coed Du was at one time rented by Cornishman John Taylor, who was responsible for building the leete in Loggerheads in about 1823. Taylor, a respected and experienced mining engineer, was employed by the Grosvenor family and during his stay he endeavoured to introduce Cornish working practices, which resulted in many industrial disputes. The house is now used as a residential home. *(Ray Davies)*

In 1829 Felix Mendelssohn visited the Taylor family who were renting Coed Du and the plaque on the wall commemorates his visit with the following words:

'Felix Mendelssohn Bartholdy
Born at Hamburg 1809, Died 1847,
Composed 'The Rivulet' in 1829,
While visiting Mr [?] Taylor,
Who rented Coed-Du,

Charles Kingsley
Born at Holme Vicarage, Devon, 1819,
Died 23rd Jany 1875,
Frequently walked along 'The Leete''

Mold has seen a great deal of development over the years, including the loss in 1999 of Dolgoed which stood on the corner of Bryn Coch Lane and Ruthin Road opposite Preswylfa. A house of real character in its own extensive grounds, it has now been replaced by a development of large detached houses. Fortunately, the large trees fronting the property have been preserved, although in summer these may have a detrimental effect on the light getting into the new homes. (Eric Keen)

Estate of the late Miss A. C, Rose Waln.

NEAR MOLD, NORTH WALES

FRON HALL

**A Substantially Built Georgian Mansion and Grounds
with Valuable Timber and Pasture Land extending in
all to approximately**

65 ACRES

For Sale by Auction
(Subject to Conditions and unless privately sold)

by

J. BRADBURNE PRICE & CO.

(Chartered Auctioneers and Estate Agents)

at

THE BLACK LION HOTEL, MOLD

ON WEDNESDAY, 2nd MAY, 1962

at 3-30 p.m.

Solicitors :
Messrs. Brown, Dobie and Rogers, 38, King Street, Chester
('Phone : Chester 25460).

Above and left: In 1665 the occupant of Fron Hall was listed as John Bythel and over the period 1701–1811, the occupants were the Williams family, three of whom were Oxford University clerics. In 1845, the Waln family took up residence and they lived in the house until 1962. Many of the older residents of the area will remember the two brothers and a sister, all of whom remained unmarried, taking an active role in the activities of the area, particularly scouting. *(Mrs Mair Bellis)*

Above and right: Until auctioned in 1973, Hafod, located on the edge of Gwernymynydd, was a private residence with the last residents being the Peyton family. Following auction, it was extensively renovated and altered and was opened as a hotel in 1978 and it continues in that role today. *(Mrs Mair Bellis)*

Left: The area had links with the 'Liverpool Trade' and in this 1967 photograph the late John D. Griffiths is seen examining a look-out tower in Hafod Road, Gwernymynydd. From his research, he believed that the seventeenth- and eighteenth-century owners of Plas Hafod were involved in the slave trade and built the look-out to watch for ships entering the Mersey Bar, Liverpool, as the river could be seen from the location. *(Rhiannon Griffiths)*

Below: Philip Davies-Cooke of Gwysaney built Llwynegrin in 1828 for his widowed stepmother. In a contemporary report it was described as a peaceful country home surrounded by 60 acres of parkland. Its many tenants included Henry Raikes, MP for Chester and Postmaster General, and for whom the nearby lane is named. Flintshire County Council now owns the hall and among its current uses it houses the register office. *(Rhiannon Griffiths)*

Above and below: Built for George Wynne in about 1724, Leeswood Hall originally had a centre section eleven bays long and two side bays with thirteen bays each. After Wynne's death in poverty, the house came into the possession of the vicar of Mold, Revd Hope Eyton, who demolished the side wings and reduced the size of the main block. The famous white gates and the black gates (the latter now at Tower) are generally believed to have been manufactured in 1726 by the Davies Brothers of Bersham, although Robert Bakewell has also been suggested as the manufacturer. *(Eric Keen)*

Penbedw Hall, located east of the village of Nannerch, was one of the first houses to have iron window frames fitted, and enjoyed a wonderful panoramic view prior to its demolition in the 1970s. Among the families living at Penbedw were the Buddicom family, who resided there from the 1800s through to the last resident, Venita Digby Buddicom. The original house on the site was linked to the Digby family, with Sir Everard being an associate of Guy Fawkes. *(Ray Davies)*

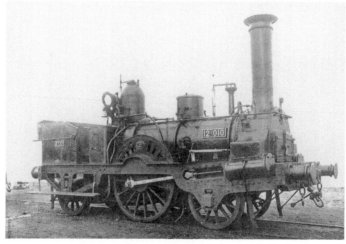

Among the family was William Barber Buddicom, a renowned Victorian railway engineer who was responsible for many of the French railways, and an example of an engine can be seen in the photograph. He was also responsible for the Liverpool Lime Street tunnels and the development of engines used in tanks. Older residents may remember a First World War tank being brought to Nannerch village where it stood until it was required for scrap in the Second World War. *(Cliff Halsall, with thanks to Flintshire Record Office)*

One of the lodges of the Penbedw Estate can be seen on the Mold to Denbigh road with the Buddicom initials still evident on the building. Although William Buddicom was a noted railway engineer, he objected to the original route of the Mold–Denbigh line on the basis that it would impact upon the view from the hall. As a result, the route was amended and an embankment provided so that he retained his unspoilt view across parkland. *(Ray Davies)*

The Pentrehobyn Estate was the site of the 2007 National Eisteddfod and the house was built around 1540 by Edward ap David ap Lloyd. Ownership has descended through generations of the same family. To the east of the house are Lletyau (lodgings) comprising a stone-roofed row of eight cells and a two-storey building for an overseer. It is believed that these were built after the dissolution of the monasteries to house poor pilgrims on their way to St Winifrede's well at Holywell. *(Ray Davies)*

Located on the outskirts of the village of Nercwys, this house was damaged by fire in the 1950s and the upper storey on the right no longer exists – yet it remains a very attractive building. In 1645, at the time of the Civil War, the vicar of Mold, George Roberts, was concerned about his safety in Mold and went to live at Plas Onn. The parish records detail his reasons; 'I baptised no more this yeare '45 neither buried any being constrained to absent myself in regard of the violence us'd in these parts then.' However, his poor curate was expected to remain! *(Ray Davies)*

The listed Plas-yn-Dre at 24 High Street is probably the last of the townhouses built by the families of the estates that ringed Mold. Built in the early to mid-eighteenth century for the Nercwys Estate, it remains known locally as Cooke and Arkwright, who were agents for a number of the local estates. The building, pictured in 1989, now houses various businesses, including WH Smith. *(Ken Lloyd Gruffydd)*

Price's Row is the only remaining example (albeit only the façade) of nineteenth-century industrial workers' houses fronting a courtyard. Built by Josiah Price, a blacksmith, they consisted of simple two up, two down houses with Price's smithy directly opposite. Visiting these houses was not without danger, particularly if any of the residents were involved in blasting works as the Local Board were concerned about miners placing the casks of gunpowder on the hearth or some other dry spot. The New Savoy Restaurant, fronting Chester Street, occupies the site. *(Ray Davies)*

Rhual is one of the major estates still existing around Mold and a house is known to have existed in the 1500s. The current house dates from 1634 and was built by Evan Edwards. It is fortunate in that it has not been materially altered through the ages and retains the original staircase as well as the great chamber over the hall entrance. The estate is now run as a dairy farm with a herd of some 300 pure Holstein cattle. *(Major B.E.P. Heaton)*

Apart from the period following the death of the heir to the estate, Major Edwin Griffith at the battle of Waterloo, the house and estate have remained in the hands of the family since at least the fourteenth century. The death of Major Griffith is commemorated with a memorial tablet in Mold parish church that states: 'On a day so fateful to his family, 18 June 1815 ... fell in the thirtieth year of his age pierced in the breast by five honourable wounds gallantly leading his Regiment, which he commanded'.

Another member of the family was to die in combat some hundred years later during the First World War. Lt-Col. Basil Philips, Commanding Officer of the 5th Battalion of the Royal Welch Fusiliers (the Flintshire Territorials), was killed during the landing at Suvla Bay in August 1915. The current owner, Major Basil Heaton, joined the Royal Artillery in 1942 and was among the first to land during the Normandy D-Day landings on 6 June 1944. We are pleased that, unlike some of his ancestors, he survived this experience. As well as military service, the family has a record of public service and Major Heaton was one of the last High Sheriffs of the old county of Flint.

Simplified Line of Descent (descent through the female line is underlined)

Evan Edwards (c.1594–1670)   = Joan Telwall of Woodford
(predeceased by son and succeeded by granddaughter)

Thomas Edwards (1625–?)   = Elizabeth Lloyd of Pentre Hobyn

Mary Edwards   = Walter Griffith of Llanfyllin

Nehemiah Griffith (1691–1738) Unmarried
(succeeded by brother)

Thomas Griffith (1695–1740)   = Jane Hughes (1706–1786)
                                                (widow of Roger Mostyn of Cilcain)

Thomas Griffith (1740–1811)   = Henrietta Maria Clarke (d.1813)

Henrietta Maria Griffith (1771–1843)   = Frederick Philips of Astley Hall

Frederick Charles Philips (1793–1858)   = Margaret Palliser

Edwin William Philips (1830–1875)   = Fanny Louisa Eyres

Basil Edwin Philips (1856–1915)   = Helena Cooke (d.1943)

Gwenllian Margaret Philips (1897–1979)   = Hugh Edward Heaton (1892–1964)

Basil Hugh Philpse Heaton (b.1923)

Right and below: It is easy to overlook many of the people who lived and worked on estates, as records generally exist only of the owner's families, but in these photographs we see Mrs Elsie Hughes (*née* Williams) who was employed as a parlour maid in the 1920s, sitting in the landscaped garden. The second photograph shows her daughter, Mrs Betty Hilditch, sitting in the same spot about seventy years later – note the garden and house remain relatively unchanged. I was privileged to be given access to the Rhual family photograph albums dating from 1800s onwards and from the prominence given to their servants in these albums, it is obvious they were held in high regard, even during difficult periods. *(Mrs Betty Hilditch)*

Although the houses pictured here in the 1950s will be easily identified by anyone driving through Sychdyn village on the Mold to Northop road, the area has since been developed and houses have been built around and also across the other side of the road. Wat's Dyke, a great earthwork, runs adjacent to the village and, along with the nearby Offa's Dyke, remains a monument to the fact that these were often violent border lands. *(Ray Davies)*

Tower is unique in that it is among the last of the castellated houses in Wales, and in 2006 BBC Wales included it in a series called *Great Houses of Wales*. In 1465 it was the home of Rheinallt ap Griffith. He had a longstanding feud with the Mayor of Chester, Roger Byrne, and when Byrne and other Chester men came to a Mold Fair, fighting broke out; Byrne was captured and hanged from a ceiling in Tower. The house is normally open to the public on bank holidays and also offers a quality B&B. *(Ray Davies)*

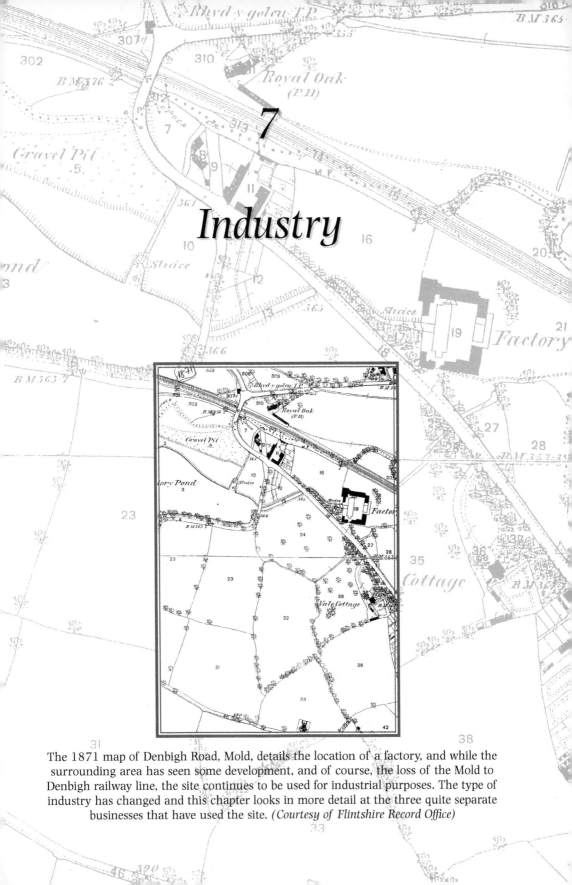

7

Industry

The 1871 map of Denbigh Road, Mold, details the location of a factory, and while the surrounding area has seen some development, and of course, the loss of the Mold to Denbigh railway line, the site continues to be used for industrial purposes. The type of industry has changed and this chapter looks in more detail at the three quite separate businesses that have used the site. *(Courtesy of Flintshire Record Office)*

Above: Built in the late 1700s by Samuel and James Knight, the cotton mill experienced great fluctuations in trade which is reflected in the numbers of people employed. In 1822, 300 workers were employed, by 1833 the mill was at a standstill, but by 1838, the workforce was almost back to the 1822 level. Disaster struck on 8 November 1866 when the building was destroyed by fire and the local newspapers reported the loss of 200 jobs. *(Ken Lloyd Gruffydd)*

Above and opposite below: The next industry to take over the site was the Alyn Tin Plate Works. The office buildings have been incorporated into the current plant and are still clearly recognisable today. Prior to its closure, it is reported to have employed around 300 workers. The company was founded in 1878–9 by Morgan Morgans and his brother-in-law, David Williams (1840–1895), both from Pontypool, and remained in their ownership until 1936 when it was sold to Richard Thomas & Co. (South Wales) before it was finally sold to Synthite in 1947. *(Ray Davies)*

Right: David Williams purchased Bromfield Hall in 1895 from lawyer W.B Marston. His daughter, Maude Williams, was a keen cyclist, and a number of photographs exist of Mold Cycling Club meeting outside Bromfield Hall. Maude married Morgan William Morgans of the Mount, Bailey Hill; a house that still exists today. *(Ray Davies)*

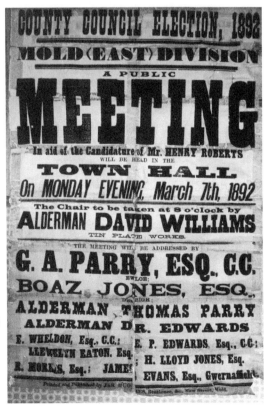

COUNTY COUNCIL ELECTION, 1892
MOLD (EAST) DIVISION
A PUBLIC
MEETING
In aid of the Candidature of Mr. HENRY ROBERTS
WILL BE HELD IN THE
TOWN HALL
On MONDAY EVENING, March 7th, 1892
The Chair to be taken at 8 o'clock by
ALDERMAN DAVID WILLIAMS
TIN PLATE WORKS
THE MEETING WILL BE ADDRESSED BY
G. A. PARRY, ESQ., C.C.
EWLOE
BOAZ JONES, ESQ.,
NERQUIS
ALDERMAN THOMAS PARRY
ALDERMAN DR. EDWARDS
E. WHELDON, Esq., C.C.; E. P. EDWARDS, Esq., C.C.;
LLEWELYN EATON, Esq.; H. LLOYD JONES, Esq.
R. MORRIS, Esq.; JAMES EVANS, Esq., Gwernaffield.
Printed and Published by J.A.R. McC. &Co., Stationers, &c., New Street, Mold.

The 6 May 1950 edition of *The Chronicle* reported on the opening of the new Synthite works with the headline, 'A shapely light industry comes to Mold...a traveller passing down the Denbigh Road today would be struck by the handsome and shapely buildings, well set out on a 36-acre site, and would be satisfied that the installations stand well against the green background, with due regard to what are described today by the vague term 'amenities.' I will leave it to the reader to decide if they have achieved their aim of 'combining industrialisation with a regard for beauty'.

The smithy at Nercwys has remained in the family since 1801 and Ted Hughes Griffiths, pictured at the top around 1960, recalled the time when dealers brought their cattle to the smithy to be shod before being driven to Smithfield Market in London for sale. The small nails were all hand forged and were the same type used for Shetland ponies. The current smith, Ian, pictured above left, travelled to Athens in support of a local member of the British Paralympic equestrian team, and in 2008 will be in charge of forty blacksmiths at the next games. *(Top and below right: Ray Davies; Below left: Glyn Hughes)*

The Bailey Hill colliery, known locally as the Bedlam pit, opened in
about 1875, but by 1893 had ceased operation, along with another
eight Mold collieries. Much of the decline was due to flooding
problems. J.D. Griffiths, in an article to a local paper, had understood
from a mining engineer that an estimated million tons of coal still
existed within a two miles radius of Mold Cross. The site is now the
home of Mold Alexandra Football Club and a housing development is
currently in the process of being built. *(Rhiannon Griffiths)*

The exact use of the (now demolished) Nercwys colliery building is
unknown but it is believed to have been an explosives or lamp store.
The Tryddyn Mill colliery first started mining in the 1840s, and to
enable the colliery to exploit its resources, it was necessary to have
a link with a railway system. A link was established with the Mold
Railway Co.'s Ffrith branch line sometime after 1859 and within a few
years it was serving six collieries, three oil works and two brickworks
at a rate of about nine trains per day. *(Ray Davies)*

Following the demise of the other Mold collieries, including Argoed, Broncoed, Bron Wylfa, Glanrafon, Mold Town, Oak Pits, Rhydygaled and Tyddyn, the Bromfield colliery was the last of the large pits to continue operation. Bromfield was producing coal in the 1850s until it finally closed in June 1916 when, in spite of extensive pumping, there was a serious danger of flooding, along with the possibility of subsidence of property, land and roads. This picture of the Bromfield Head shaft was taken in about 1960 prior to the development of the Bromfield trading estate. In the background is the town gasholder. *(Ray Davies)*

In addition to extensive coalmining, lead mines abounded in the area and the Siglen Isa mine in Gwernymynydd can be seen in this early 1900s view from the Glyndwr Road. Silica stone was also quarried and the quarry behind the Rainbow pub yielded the stone used in Lever Brothers famous product Vim. This continued until the late 1950s when demand for silica fell and the quarry no longer produced the white stone required. *(Ray Davies)*

Driving down Padeswood Road towards Mold, it is difficult to believe that the agricultural landscape and golf courses on the left were once heavily industrialised areas. In 1857 Padeswood and nearby Llong had an iron works, chemical works, two oil works and numerous collieries, including three named Hop, Skip and Jump. It is believed thousands worked in the area, which is crisscrossed by a maze of public footpaths enabling workers to travel from surrounding towns and villages. *(Ray Davies)*

Apart from flooding being a significant negative factor in mines, water was also a source of power for other industries and waterwheels are still a common sight, as can be seen from the very attractive house converted from Llanferres mill on the River Alyn near Loggerheads Country Park. The River Alyn rises near Llandegla and enters Flintshire just below Loggerheads and at one point in the park it often – in dry weather – disappears into a subterranean passage leaving the riverbed completely dry. *(Ray Davies)*

Right: A 1796 print of the area indicates that the Loggerheads Pentre Mill was on the site at that time but the building we see today is of a later, unknown date. Water was diverted from the River Alyn over a weir and through a sluice gate to enter the mill-race and onto the millpond, eventually flowing through a cast-iron flume and into the buckets on the wheel. The flour and cattle feed derived from the milled grain is likely to have been sold in the market towns of Mold and Ruthin. The grinding of wheat for bread stopped in the 1920s, but the grinding of barley and oats for cattle feed continued until the 1940s.*(Eric Keen)*

Below: The mill in the early 1900s. Until the 1940s, it was also used as a sawmill by William Williams, with the water-wheel providing power to a saw blade for cutting tree trunks. A small tramway was constructed to assist with the movement of the timber. Williams lived in Sawmills Cottage, which can be seen in the centre of the picture. *(Ray Davies)*

The Glan Alyn lead mine stood close to the mill and was operating before 1870. Signs of such industrial activity can still be seen in the Loggerheads Country Park and the ruins of the building in the left of the photograph are all that remain of an engine house. During the nineteenth century the population around Loggerheads and nearby villages and hamlets grew as lead mining activities increased. *(Eric Keen)*

This 8-ton Aveling and Porter steamroller, driven by its joint owner, Eric Croall, is named 'Unbelievable' and was built in 1920. It started its working life for Watford Urban District Council and changed hands several times before coming into the possession of Eric Croall and Dave Burgess. A common sight at fêtes and other shows throughout the area, it also provided transport for Father Christmas each year. Sadly, Eric died at a relatively young age and the steamroller has now left the area. *(Eric Croall)*

8

Sport & Leisure

Long before the concept of Premier Leagues, European competitions and millionaire players, football was played in all sorts of conditions, and in this picture we see a 1912 match between Liverpool and Gwernymynydd played in the small village just outside Mold. The result is not known and the absence of nets and solid wooden goalposts, along with a crowd in suits, collars and ties and of course caps, tells of a time when attending football matches did not require independent financial means. *(Ray Davies)*

The Management Committee

request the pleasure of the Company of

Two members of the Glee Party.

at the OPENING CEREMONY

of the Gwernymynydd Village Hall

on SATURDAY, 15th December, 1934,

at 3 p.m.

R.S.V.P. to the Secretary,
Hamadan, Gwernymynydd.

Above and below: Gwernymynydd village hall had a variety of homes and, as can be seen from the invitation, a new hall was opened on 15 December 1934 in the building that has subsequently been tastefully converted into a bungalow. The village centre now operates out of what was previously the old primary school, and in 2007, the organisations using the village centre included a playgroup, Cubs, Mountain Harmony Group, adult and children's exercise groups, Mold Alex Football Club, a Women's Institute, a youth club and the Mold Christian Fellowship. *(Mrs Mair Bellis)*

Children's " RADIO STAR " Competitions.

Hear your Children perform through the Microphone ! !

Class.

1. Best Vocalist under 10 years   ...   ...   Prize 5/-
2. Best Vocalist, 10—15 years   ...   ...   do.
3. Best Recitation under 12 years   ...   ...   do.
   (not to exceed 2 minutes)
4. Best Instrumental Solo (children up to 14 years)   do.

(Competitors in Classes 1 and 2 to perform unaccompanied).

ENTRANCE FEE (All Classes) - 6d. each.

ENTRIES to : The Headmaster, Council School, Mold, or
The Headmaster, Central School, Mold.

Closing Date : 22nd September, 1944.

———————❖———————

LADIES' ANKLE COMPETITION.

Competitors to Parade at 4 p.m. on the Field.

Prizes : (1) Pair of Fully Fashioned Silk Stockings ;
(2) Pair of Silk Stockings.

ENTRANCE FEE - 1/-   Entries to Mrs. Challinor,
High Street, Mold.

———————❖———————

GRAND NOVELTY ' LUCKY DIP ' COMPETITION.

First Prize : Gold Sovereign.   Over 50 other Prizes.

———————❖———————

Supporting Side-Shows and Displays.

———————❖———————

Refreshments Provided at Moderate Charges.

RED CROSS and ST. JOHN

————❖————

' Victory Garden ' Week

At MOLD

September 23–30, 1944

————❖————

PROGRAMME OF

Special Events & Attractions

At the Alun County School

(by kind permission of the Governors),

On Saturday, September 23rd

————❖————

Admission to Field   -   1/-

(Children and Members of the Forces in Uniform, 6d.)

PROGRAMME   -   THREEPENCE.

J. H. Edwards, Ltd., Printers, &c., Mold.

Above, left and right: The 'Victory Garden' week had a full programme of events and attractions including the Home Guard Band and 'Courtessa' dancing troupe, a baby show, a dog show, a children's 'Radio Star' competition, a Grand Novelty 'Lucky Dip' competition with the first prize of a gold sovereign, as well as other supporting sideshows and displays. However, in these days of political correctness, it is unlikely that the 'Ladies' Ankle' competition will be repeated and I am not in a position to judge whether the first prize of a pair of fully fashioned silk stockings would still attract entries. *(Rhiannon Griffiths)*

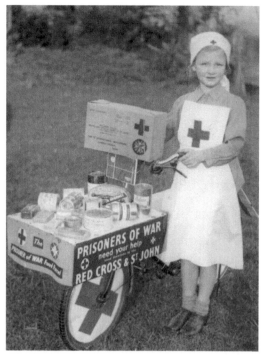

As part of the Victory Garden Week Grand Parade through the town, various competitions were held, including 'best tableaux on conveyance', 'best decorated pram' and 'most original gentleman'. Depending upon the competition, an entrance fee of between 6d and 1s was payable. A monetary prize was awarded for the 'best in class' and here we see Rhiannon Griffiths, who won 10s for the best decorated bicycle with her mock-up of a prisoners of war food parcel. Rhiannon remembers being so tired after walking through the town that she had to be given a lift back on the Red Cross float. *(Rhiannon Griffiths)*

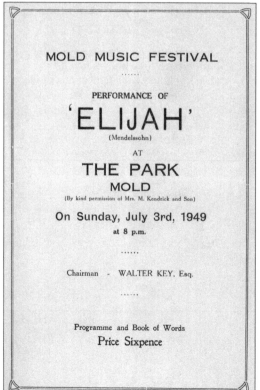

The programme for the 1949 Mold Music Festival is typical of the many cultural events held in Mold. One of the stars of the festival, held at The Park, was the internationally renowned bass, Owen Brannigan. Among the cultural organisations were a town orchestra, various bands, choirs and drama groups, and while many of these no longer exist, Clwyd Theatr Cymru continues to provide a full programme of events.

Right and below: In the small village of Rhydymwyn can be found the Second World War valley site where chemical weapons were manufactured and early work on the atomic bomb was carried out. Adjacent to the site is a small industrial estate that had previously been a racetrack with both motorcycle and car races organised by Wirral Hundred Motor Club. The events were held under FIA and RAC rules and today it is difficult to imagine an E-type Jaguar hurtling around such a small area.

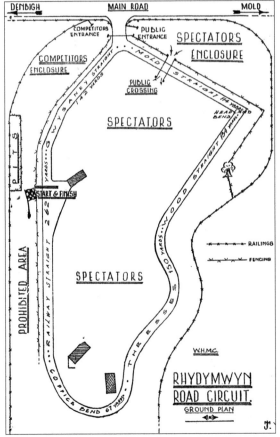

Mold Alexandra Football Club

Newsletter

Summer 1999

Welcome to the Mold Alex FC Summer 1999 Newsletter. The aim of this Newsletter is to update our sponsors and supporters of the activities of the Club over the past year both on and off the park. The past twelve months have been very eventful and encouraging for the future of the Club and we are looking to move forward into the next century and build on seventy years of history.

Promotion

Mold Alex FC started the 1998/99 season in the Welsh National League Division One, our lowest league position for many years and our immediate aim was promotion to the Premier Division. Under the management of Steve Griffith the team of locally based players achieved their goal with a game to spare. We eventually finished the season in second place losing only five league matches all season. The team has effectively been together since the ages of 11/12 and has graduated through the Mold Alex Youth set up. Steve has added a small number of experienced player to his squad and can be very pleased with their performances over the season including ten straight wins from the opening day of the season.

Ground Developments

Mold Alex play at Alyn Park in the Maes-y-Dre area of the town and have done since their formation in 1929. Although the ground has suffered from vandalism in recent years the Club have continued to improve facilities at Alyn Park in recent years. In the Autumn of 1998 we were able to secure two portacabins from Vauxhall Motors in Ellesmere Port. We have now

converted the first cabin into the Alex Cafe, a facility offering hot and cold drinks on match days and also providing shelter from the elements in the Winter. The funding of this development was assisted by a grant of #250 from Mold Town Council. We have also extended the car park behind the goal with aggregate donated by local company Pioneer. Over the summer we are building two new dugouts on opposite sides of the pitch for the home and visiting teams. The ground also has seated accommodation for 100+ and a sizeable covered standing area. We hope be able to use the floodlights again next winter.

Sponsorship

Over the past few years we have been honoured to have Synthite Ltd

Kevin Ratcliffe and Neville Southall pictured with
Alex Secretary Gareth Hampson and Manager Steve Griffith

as our Club's main sponsors. The Company are also our landlords and have assisted Mold Alex in numerous ways in recent years. We wear the Synthite name on our blue home kit and in 1998 we were donated a red change kit from Padeswood Company Castle Cement. Our match programme in

crammed with adverts from small local business' and we are grateful for all the support we have received from our Club sponsors.

Other Activities

During the 1998/99 season we had the honour of welcoming the Wales A squad to Alyn Park for a training session prior to their match against Northern Ireland at Wrexham. The squad contained a number of full internationals and was coached by Neville Southall and Kevin Ratcliffe. We also hosted a training session for Wycombe Wanderers FC the day before they played against Wrexham FC. Wycombe manager and FA Cup Final scorer Lawrie Sanchez was most impressed by the quality of the facilities and the playing service. Alyn Park also hosted three

Deeside Sunday League Finals and for the first time the annual Mold Fireworks Evening organised by the North Wales Fire Service. This event was a great success and an estimated 1500/2000 adults and children were in attendance.

Published by The Committee of Mold Alexandra Football Club

Mold Alexandra was formed in 1929 with its home ground on the site of Bailey Hill colliery at Alyn Park. The ground has also been used for training sessions by professional teams. During the 1998–9 season, the Welsh A Squad used the ground prior to their match against Northern Ireland at Wrexham's racecourse ground. Pictured are the Wales Management team, ex-Everton and Wales favourites Kevin Ratcliffe and Neville Southall, along with officials of Mold Alex. (*Colin Hampson*)

Mold has a good tradition of sport encouraged by local schools, and as well as football, the town has many other sports clubs too numerous to mention, but including rugby, cricket, golf, swimming, badminton, tennis and general fitness. Mold also hosts the annual Flintshire 10k Road Race and in 2003, this incorporated the Welsh National and Inter Regional Championships in this field, which included a number of Kenyan athletes.

Bowls has always been a popular leisure and competitive activity and the town still boasts a number of bowling clubs. This early 1900s picture shows bowls on the Bailey Hill green. In past generations, several private bowling clubs operated, with one at the rear of the Dolphin pub which now contains one of the town's car parks. In Wrexham Street, the shop of D.M. Jones can be found, which was originally the Bowling Green Hotel, with the green located at the rear. *(Ray Davies)*

The Magazine of 1378 (Mold) Squadron Air Training Corps

Lord Lieutenant's Cadets

Another First for Mold

Over the years Mold Squadron has had a number of cadets appointed as Lord Lieutenant's Cadets, but never before have we seen two cadets selected consecutively.

The picture opposite shows Flt. Sgt. Geraint Kingman receiving his Certificate of Appointment from the Lord Lieutenant, Trefor Jones Esq CBE, at Boddelwythan Castle on the Thursday 15th March.

The picture below shows Sgt Adam Smith receiving his Badge of Office for the coming year. The badge is worn on uniform to signify that the wearer is an appointed Lord Lieutenant's Cadet.

Each year the Lord Lieutenant personally presents these items to his appointed cadets. Representatives of the cadet's family or friends, and a representative of the Squadron, usually the CO, are also invited to the proceedings. The recommendation for appointment made by the CO is read out during the ceremony, and the presentations are made. The badge of office is presented at the beginning of the year of appointment, whilst the Certificate is presented on satisfactory completion of the year of service as a Lord Lieutenant's Cadet.

It is a considerable honour to be appointed, because appointments are not made by the Corps but by the Lord Lieutenant. As the Lord Lieutenant is the Queens representative in the County the honour is particu-

Continued on Page 9

INSIDE		
Duke of Edinburgh's Award	Pages	14 - 19
Nordic Skiing - well almost !	Pages	20 - 22
A sickening experience	Page	23
The Cadet CV	Page	26

Magazine sponsored by: **Sir y Fflint Flintshire** COUNTY COUNCIL for support given during the Flintshire 10k Run

Mold has always had a proud tradition of youth organisations but sadly, due to the lack of willing adult leaders, a number of these have disappeared from the scene. Thankfully, the 1378 (Mold) Squadron Air Training Corps does not fall into this category, and from the Combined Cadet Centre they share with the RWF Army Cadets, they have a full programme of activities, including providing valuable assistance at many community activities. Open to both boys and girls, the squadron strength on 31 March 2007 stood at forty-three enrolled cadets. *(Flt-Lt Tim Kingman)*

Right: The National Eisteddfod can be traced back to 1176 when, under the patronage of the Lord Rhys, an event was held at his castle in Cardigan, where invited poets and musicians from all over the country competed. The best musician and poet were awarded a 'chair' at the Lord's table and the terminology remains in use today. In 1568, an Eisteddfod was held in the Flintshire town of Caerwys, and in 1880, the National Eisteddfod Association was formed and given the responsibility to stage an annual festival.

Below: Mold has hosted the National Eisteddfod on four separate occasions: 1873, 1923, 1991 and 2007. Pictured is the proclamation ceremony held on Bailey Hill for the 1991 Eisteddfod, with the actual cultural festival taking place on the Rhual Estate. The proclamation is given a year in advance, when those wishing to participate are invited to attend the following year. The Eisteddfod is an eight-day celebration of Welsh culture, including arts and crafts, music, dance and poetry, and attracts around 6,000 competitors and 160,000 visitors. *(Brian Pollard)*

Eisteddfod Genedlaethol Cymru, Mold, 1923.

Exhibition of Arts and Crafts.

Catalogue.

CROSVILLE TEA HOUSE & GARDENS, LOGGERHEADS.

Originally part of the nearby Colomendy Estate, the Loggerheads Country Park, as it is now called, was sold in 1926 to the Crossville Motor Co. who developed the area and ran regular services from Merseyside. When we consider the very high volume of traffic now using the roads, I wonder what the 1824 visitor who complained that 'vehicles on the new turnpike road, at a rate of several a day thereby spoiling the rural simplicity and quiet seclusion of the park' would think? *(Ray Davies)*

Taken on an autumn day in 1995, this prize-winning picture called 'The Woodland Walker' symbolises for many what the country park and the Leete walk is all about – natural beauty and solitude (other than on warm Sunday afternoons), and all derived from what was an industrial area. The park remains popular with locals, as well as attracting large numbers of visitors from Merseyside and beyond. *(Eric Keen)*

Guaranteed to bring a sigh of nostalgia among the older residents, the Savoy cinema, located in Chester Street, was built in the 1920s and was Mold's first purpose-built cinema. Fred Roberts of Bryn Awel designed the building and, following approval by the Medical Officer of Health and the Inspector of Nuisances, the plans were passed. The cinema finally closed in 1972 to allow for the building of the telephone exchange. (*Ray Davies*)

The author, pictured above Llanarmon yn Ial with his two Welsh Border Collies, Seren on the right and Brân on the left, both taking a great interest in the flock of sheep at the bottom of the hill. The beautiful scenery with the series of fishing lakes is typical of the hills of the area but it belies the fact that this was, and continues to be, an industrial area. While the metal mines have now all closed, quarrying continues and one can just be seen in the far distance in the centre of the picture. (*Judith Rowe*)

Moel Fammau is the highest point of the Clwydian hills and the jubilee tower on the summit was built by public subscription in 1810 to commemorate the fiftieth anniversary of George III's accession to the throne, but during a great storm in 1862, it collapsed. Efforts were made in 1882 to restore the monument to celebrate Queen Victoria's jubilee but insufficient funds were raised. A fraction of its original size, the ruins were finally tidied up in 1970 to commemorate the investiture of Prince Charles as Prince of Wales in 1969. *(Eric Keen)*

9

People

John Blackwell (1797–1840) was born in this house in Ponterwyl, Mold, and as a boy, attended the nearby Welsh Calvinistic Methodist Church. At the age of eleven, he was apprenticed to the shoemaker William Kirkham, who encouraged the young John to follow literary pursuits, and in 1823, he won an Eisteddfod chair prize using the Bardic name Alun. While he had had little formal education, his abilities were recognised by local notables and with their financial aid, he was able to attend Oxford University. After graduation, he was ordained in the Anglican Church, but sadly died at the early age of forty-three. *(Rhiannon Griffiths)*

Ystrad Alun

Nadolig
2003
Christmas

John Ambrose Lloyd (1815-1874)
Composer and Musician

JOURNAL OF THE MOLD CIVIC SOCIETY
CYLCHGRAWN CYMDEITHAS DDINESIG YR WYDDGRUG

High on the wall of Barclays Bank in the High Street is a plaque in Welsh that translates as follows: 'In this house was born John Ambrose Lloyd (1815–1874), musician and composer'. Lloyd left Mold in 1830 to join his brother Isaac, a teacher in Liverpool, where he attended the Tabernacle Chapel and formed a choir. He began composing hymns while working at the Mechanics' Institute where he established the Liverpool Welsh Choral Society. *(Mold & District Civic Society)*

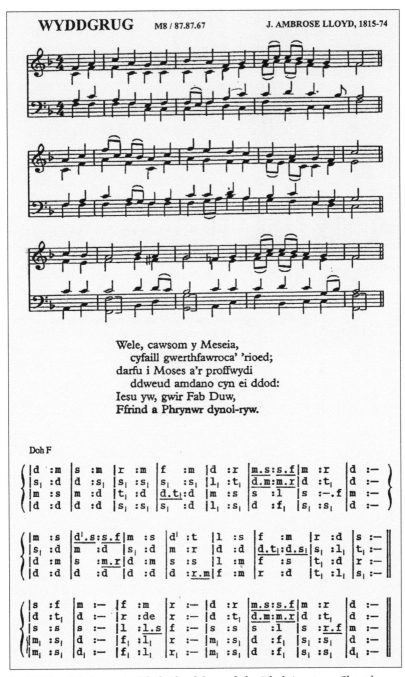

WYDDGRUG M8 / 87.87.67 J. AMBROSE LLOYD, 1815-74

Wele, cawsom y Meseia,
cyfaill gwerthfawroca' 'rioed;
darfu i Moses a'r proffwydi
ddweud amdano cyn ei ddod:
Iesu yw, gwir Fab Duw,
Ffrind a Phrynwr dynol-ryw.

In 1864, while living in Rhyl, Lloyd formed the Rhyl Amateur Choral Society. Many of his hymn tunes were named after north-east Wales place names and 'Wyddgrug' (the Welsh name for Mold) was written when he was sixteen years of age. He published his many tunes in a number of books and is recognised as a great hymn writer with a prolific output. This included ninety-two hymns, twenty-eight anthems and three cantatas.
(Mold & District Civic Society)

Daniel Owen (1836–1895) was the youngest of six children and is often described as the Welsh Charles Dickens. In 1837, his father and two brothers (one of whom was only ten years old) were killed in a flooding disaster at the Argoed colliery. At the age of twelve, Owen was apprenticed to a tailor where his fellow workers were well versed and his all-round education blossomed. At twenty-nine, he entered Bala Theological College but returned to Mold to take care of his mother and was never ordained, although he continued to preach while working as a tailor. *(Ray Davies)*

Owen continued to enhance his reputation as a novelist with stories based on a chapel-dominated town at a time of great industrial and agricultural change, and his memory lives on, not just in the famous statue by Goscombe John, but also in buildings and various commemorative events. This photograph shows children in national costume beside his statue when it was in its original location in Hall Fields. The statue has now been relocated to a position outside the library in Earl Road (*see* page 103) and the library itself contains an excellent Daniel Owen exhibition that is worth the reader taking time to visit. *(Ray Davies)*

Right: The tailor's shop, pictured here in the 1960s, was originally owned by Owen and is now part of the Y Pentan public house. Daniel Owen not only continued to be closely linked with the Bethesda Chapel but he also took full part in community life and was the first chairman of Mold Urban District Council in 1894. *(Rhiannon Griffiths)*

Below: The We Three Loggerheads public house may seem a strange inclusion in a chapter on people, but it has a direct link with Richard Wilson (1714–1782), considered to be foremost among British landscape painters. The original inn sign was reputedly painted by Wilson to pay for his not inconsiderable bar bill, and depicts two heads with the viewer being the third person. *(Edward Roberts)*

Left: Richard Wilson was born in Penegroes, near Machynlleth, to a poor clergyman, but as his mother was related to the Wynne family of Leeswood Hall, he spent his childhood in Mold. Sponsored by his uncle, George Wynne, Wilson went to Italy in 1750 and studied both in Venice and Rome during a six-year stay. During his stay he met fellow artists, including Vernet and Zuccarelli, and had the opportunity to mix with the upper echelons of Italian society.

Below: On his return to the UK, Wilson became a founding member of the Royal Academy, but as tastes changed, he found it more difficult to sell his pictures, and in 1776, his friends found him employment as the Academy's librarian at a salary of £50 per annum. However, in 1781 he returned to his aunt's home at Colomendy Hall, near Mold, where he continued to paint in-between regular visits to local hostelries. He died in 1782 and was buried in St Mary's churchyard where his grave is marked by a Mold Civic Society plaque. A plaque and memorial window can also be found inside the church. *(Eric Keen)*

MOLD CIVIC SOCIETY

The Tomb of Richard Wilson, 1713 - 1782

A portrait and landscape artist and one of the founders of the Royal Academy, regarded by many as the father of British landscape painting. Born at Penegoes, near Machynlleth, he was related to the Wynne family of Leeswood Hall and he spent much of his childhood in the area. He studied in London under Thomas Wright and later spent time in Venice and Rome, where he gained a reputation as a landscape artist. He returned to London and travelled widely through England and Wales, painting many familiar scenes. He became Librarian at the RA before ill health and reduced circumstances forced him to return to live with a cousin at Colomendy Hall, near Mold.

Beddgist Richard Wilson, 1713 - 1782

Arlunydd portreadau a thirluniau ac un o sylfaenwyr yr Academi Frenhinol, a gyfrifir gan lawer yn dad tirlunio Prydeinig. Ei eni ym Mhenegoes, ger Machynlleth. Roedd ganddo berthynas deuluol â Wynneiaid Plas Coed-llai, a threuliodd lawer o'i blentyndod yn yr ardal. Astudiodd yn Llundain o dan Thomas Wright, ac yn ddiweddarach bu am gyfnod yn Fenis a Rhufain, lle yr enillodd enw fel tirlunydd. Dychwelodd i Lundain a theithiodd yn helaeth yng Nghymru a Lloegr, gan baentio llawer o olygfeydd cyfarwydd. Daeth yn Llyfrgellydd yr Academi Frenhinol ; yna fe'i gorfodwyd gan salwch a thlodi i ddychwelyd i fyw gyda chyfnither ym Mlas Colomendy, ger Yr Wyddgrug.

CYMDEITHAS DDINESIG YR WYDDGRUG

Pictured is the military funeral of Walter Whitley (1895–1918) who lived with his parents at Ffynnonfa Cottage, Maes-y-Dre, Mold. Prior to his Royal Marines call up in 1916, Whitley had worked as a furnace man at the Alyn Tinplate Works. He was seriously wounded while aboard HMS *Vindictive* during the battle of Zeebrugge and finally died of his wounds in the Royal Naval Hospital, Chatham. An exhibit is dedicated to Whitley in the Town Library Museum. *(Ray Davies)*

No chapter on local people would be complete without a photograph of Mold residents going about their normal business on market day. This photograph was taken in May 2007 during the BBC Wales filming of *Jamie and Derek's Big Weekend*, centred around Mold. Jamie Owen, newsreader and presenter, is to the left of the trio, masking the author, and Derek Brockway, weatherman, is to the right. *(Eric Keen)*

In Chapter 6 we came across Henry Raikes at Llwynegrin, but another member of the Raikes family also has a claim to fame. Although not a resident of Mold, Robert Raikes is acknowledged as the founder of Sunday schools. The 1880 medal was struck to commemorate the centenary of the establishment of Sunday schools. *(Rhiannon Griffiths)*

10

Public Service

A single storey Assembly Hall was built in 1845 on the site of the old leet courthouse of the Manor of Mold, which had previously been the site of the Assizes. In 1874, a second storey was added which housed a library administered by the Mold Cosmopolitan Society. An 1876 trade directory describes the building thus: 'The new Market hall, which is chiefly used for the sale of Butcher's meat, is the property of a private company, and has a very central position. Over the market is a fine assembly room suitable for entertainments.' *(Rhiannon Griffiths)*

A further floor was added to the Assembly Hall in the late 1870s and in the 1920s the second floor housed the Mold Kinema Co. with the projector being powered by a generator. Patrons would sit on benches to watch silent movies that were accompanied by a pianist. The late Victor Harley remembers watching a film about the First World War where yellow filters were used to simulate a gas attack. Later, the third floor was used as a venue for dances and other entertainment, with The Beatles appearing in 1962. *(Glynn Morris)*

Mold was the home of the Flintshire Yeomanry Cavalry, Mold Troop, whose commissioned officers in 1838 were comprised of the following: Captain John Wynne-Eyton, Leeswood Hall; Edward Pemberton (Cornet), Plas Isaf; Lt-Col. Frederick C. Phillips, Rhual; Pyers Mostyn (Cornet), Talacre. The troop was also comprised of nine NCOs and forty-four privates. By 1876, two military units were based in Mold: First Flintshire, at the pictured barracks, and the Flintshire Volunteers in the High Street. *(Ray Davies)*

Erected on the site of the town's old lock-ups, the old County Buildings housed the offices of Flintshire County Council before the county administration moved to the new Shire Hall in 1967. The large doors of the central building previously housed the militia and were strengthened with steel to withstand possible attacks by Fenians or even rebellious local miners. *(Ray Davies)*

Built around 1881 by Lockwood, the old police station in Chester Street is now used by Flintshire County Council. In the 1950s, this was the headquarters of Flintshire Constabulary with the wonderfully evocative telephone number of Mold 321. The building is now called Ty Terrig (Terrig House) and is used for a variety of educational functions as well as housing the Citizens Advice Bureau. *(Rhiannon Griffiths)*

The Flintshire Police contingent for the Coronation of Queen Elizabeth II pictured outside the old courthouse. From left to right, front row: Spt J. Edwards (Deputy Chief Constable), Fenlli Roberts (Chief Constable), Inspector H.I. Williams. Second row: PC J. Williams, PC J. Taylor, Sgt B Roberts, Spt Constable C. Roberts, Sgt J.E. Jones, PC J. Edwards, PC R. Lloyd. Third row: -?-, PC J. Challinor, PC E. Roberts. Fourth row: PC C. Proctor, PC W. Blackwell, PC T. Rowlands, PC M. Huxley. Back row: PC B. Davies, PC G. Jones, PC E. Young. *(Paul Davies, with kind permission of North Wales Police)*

The old courthouse, built from sandstone, was completed in 1834 and was erected to accommodate the meetings of the Quarter sessions and Assize courts previously held at the Leet Court on the Cross. Subsequently, Mold Town colliery sank shafts nearby, undermining the building and causing extensive damage. The courthouse was the location of the miners' trial, which resulted in the previously described Mold Riots. Much altered in 1880, the building is currently unused, although hopes are high that funds may become available to use the building as a permanent town museum. *(Rhiannon Griffiths)*

Mold was split into sections for Civil Defence Wardens. Pictured is the group based at the Wrexham Street post opposite the old Baptist church (seen at the rear of the photograph). From left to right, back row: Cecil Goodwin, -?-, Ronald Edwards, Llewelyn Griffiths, George Thomas, John David Griffiths. From left to right, front row: George Allen, Hywel Roberts (bakehouse), Morgan Jones (bakehouse driver), Algy Elwyn, Tom Kinsey (tripe shop). *(Rhiannon Griffiths)*

One air-raid shelter remains at the top of Clayton Road and another at the rear of the Parish Hall but no other signs of the Second World War remain in the town, including the siren that was mounted on top of the Assembly Hall. The precautions were necessary as the aircraft factory at Broughton, the Valley Works at Rhydymwyn and steelworks were prime targets and the area was probably a secondary target if the bombers had been unable to offload their bombs over Liverpool. *(Eric Keen)*

Above and below: The old cottage hospital in Pwll Glas was built in 1877 and was ultimately replaced by a new hospital in 1984, though the building remains in use by the Health Authority. The North Wales Nursing Association was formed in 1910, and because patients had to pay for their services, funding was often a problem for the locally employed nurses. The birth of the NHS in 1948 removed the need for such bodies but Leeswood & Pontblyddyn Association did not finalise their account until 1970. *(Ray Davies)*

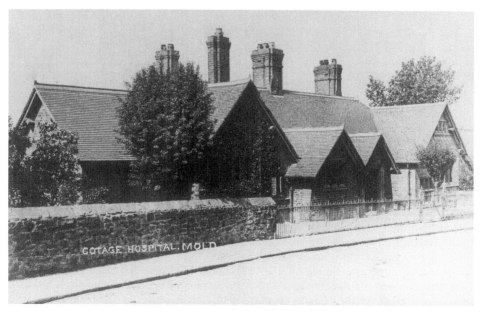

Pictured in 2004 is the modern library (which also houses a small museum and gallery) with the Daniel Owen statue in the front. The town library has had a number of homes over the years including one run by the Cosmopolitan Society in the Assembly Hall and in a 1876 trade directory, the library and reading room are shown as being at No. 15 High Street. The office next to the Victoria in Chester Street was also used as the County Library with the well-known character Ned Harries as County Librarian. *(Glynn Morris)*

Designed by Fred Roberts of Bryn Awel, the Town Hall in Earl Road was built in 1911 as a gift from Peter Roberts of Bromfield Hall, Mold, and a dedication stone on the front of the building records this fact. During the First World War, the Town Hall also housed the munitions office, and in the Second World War, the food office. Mold Urban District Council continued to use the building until Local Government Reorganisation in 1974. *(Glynn Morris)*

Prior to the building of the fire station in Lead Mills, this station was previously located in King Street, but due to the demands of the modern-day service, a new purpose-built building was necessary. Mold station is part of the North Wales Fire and Rescue Service and is a retained station whereby firemen follow their normal occupations and are mobilised by pager in the event of a fire. The station has a proud tradition of fundraising for charity, including the pictured carwash and a 5th of November firework display. *(Eric Keen)*

Pictured outside Flintshire County Council Offices in Hall Fields, the fire brigade of the 1930s is a totally different organisation from today's Fire and Rescue Service, not least in the types of incidents today's firemen are expected to deal with. How much protection the uniforms and beautifully polished helmets seen on the top of the appliance gave the wearer is not known but these were often seen in various parades and on formal occasions. *(Ray Davies)*

The rear of the fire and ambulance stations can be seen in this 1998 picture taken from the old railway bridge in King Street during the construction of the Aldi supermarket and McDonalds. The cars in the foreground are parked on the site of the old Mold to Denbigh railway line and, as can be seen on page 122, is an area susceptible to flooding. *(Eric Keen)*

Seen from the top of St Mary's Curch tower is the white County Hall (formerly Shire Hall) in the centre of the photograph, which replaced the old County Buildings in Hall Fields and was officially opened by HRH Princess Margaret on 29 May 1968. To the left of the County Hall is the brick-built Clwyd Theatre Cymru, containing the Emlyn Williams and Anthony Hopkins theatres as well as a cinema and other function rooms. The theatre runs a programme of high quality productions, as well as promoting children's and youth activities. *(Eric Keen)*

Mold and district has always had a proud tradition of military service, as is evident from the many memorials and cenotaphs located in churches and villages throughout the area. Pictured is the Airborne Regiment's veterans' parade held in Mold on 16 August 1998 when the salute was taken by General Anthony Farrar-Hockley (1924–2006), who ran away from school to enlist at the outbreak of the Second World War, and in the 1970s commanded the land forces in Northern Ireland. *(Eric Keen)*

A local person associated with the Parachute Regiment is Captain Nicholas Archdale of Penbedw, near Nannerch, who served in the 7th Parachute Battalion, with one of his fellow officers being the well-known actor Richard Todd. Their target on D-Day was to secure the important Pegasus Bridge across the Orne Caen Canal, thereby preventing the Germans from bringing reinforcements to the beachheads. *(Eric Keen)*

This 1930s picture of the cemetery brings us a view one would not see today as the chapel has been demolished and a car park has replaced this wonderful building. Daniel Owen is buried in the cemetery and his grave is signposted for those wishing to visit it. One of Daniel Owen's earliest writings followed a visit to Richard Wilson's grave in St Mary's churchyard. The rough English translation is: 'Ah, Wilson and is this your lowly grave? / So unadorned it is, in aspect foul.' *(Rhiannon Griffiths)*

The old county gaol in Upper Bryn Coch Lane was erected in 1870 at a cost of £25,133 1s 9d and replaced the gaol in Flint. It was closed in 1878 when the Home Office took over control of prisons. An early report highlights how things have changed: 'There is accommodation for 95 prisoners but crime being almost unknown in this part of the County, it is very seldom more than one fifth of the cells are occupied.' *(Rhiannon Griffiths)*

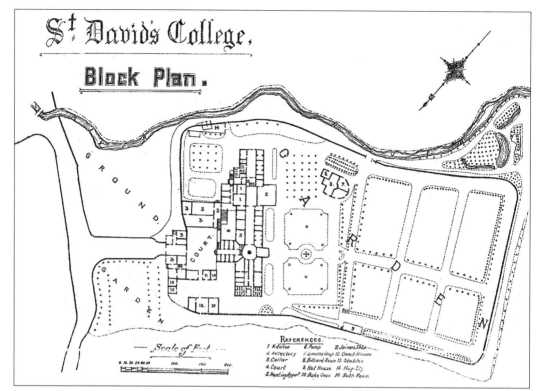

In 1881 the gaol was sold to French Jesuit priests who used it as a training college and, as can be seen from the block diagram, renamed it St David's College. In their 1889 guidebook, M.J.B. Baddeley and C.S. Ward noted its existence with the following; 'the number of clerically dressed trios taking their daily constitutional and speaking any language but English, will suggest to us that it is in a flourishing condition'. *(Rhiannon Griffiths)*

11

Schools

Like most of the local villages, Nercwys had its own school from the nineteenth century onwards, and Bonc yr Ysgol catered for many children whose fathers and older siblings would have been employed in the mining industry. In an 1886 inspection report, Abraham Thomas was less than impressed with the teacher, a shoemaker, or the pupils whom he described as 'heavy and dull'. He was particularly concerned that the girls were receiving no tuition in needlework. *(Ray Davies)*

The gable end of the building seen on the left of the picture is the first purpose-built school in the village of Cilcain. Now a private home, an inscription on the building records its previous use: 'This building was erected on the Common by a voluntary subscription from the Landowners and Occupiers of Land in the Parish as a School for the use and benefit of Parishioners 1799'. *(Ray Davies)*

During a visit to Gwernaffield in 1869, C.H. Leslie included the following description of the school in his book *Rambles around Mold*: 'And hark! What is that comes cheerily on this scene where we thought we were wandering in loneliness? 'Tis the sweet voice of innocent childhood being dismissed from the school at Gwernaffield'. As well as the pleasure of dealing with such children, the teacher had this very desirable house in which to live. *(J. Penrith)*

The National School at Halkyn was built in 1849 by the Marquis of Westminster (forefather of the Duke of Westminster) at a cost of £1,408 19s 5d and comprised two rooms, one for boys and the other for girls. The building was then enlarged in 1898–9. In a Charity Commissioners report of 1847, mention is made of the large influx of English miners, changing the area from being almost exclusively Welsh speaking. *(Ray Davies)*

This tree brought down by the great winds of January 2007 provides the foreground to the Alun School and sports centre swimming pool. The Alun School also shares the site with the other Mold secondary school, the Welsh Medium Maes Garmon, named after the field in which the Alleluia victory took place. A further secondary school is located in Mynydd Isa, and Catholic pupils travel to St Richard Gwyn in Flint. *(Eric Keen)*

The old British School in Glanrafon was built around 1845 and replaced a Welsh Medium School run in the Bethesda Chapel vestry. Later renamed the Board School, Bryn Coch CP and subsequently, the Welsh medium Ysgol Glanrafon, it is now used as a drama centre and the Master's house is used by the BBC, although at the time of writing, the Eisteddfod office is based in the building. *(Ray Davies)*

Pupils of Ysgol Bryn Gwalia and the iconic St Mary's parish church provide the backdrop to a visit by HRH the Princess Royal in February 2005 when she made an official visit to Mold Community Hospital. However, prior to her departure by helicopter she made time to talk to pupils and staff at the school. *(Eric Keen)*

The National School or The Voluntary Primary (VP) School in King Street was built in 1849 with the right-hand section being the caretaker's house. One of the incumbents was Mrs Betty Hilditch whom we met previously in the garden at Rhual (*see* page 65). To the right of the school is St Mary's church hall, consecrated in 1878 as St John's Anglican Church and built for the use of Welsh-speaking Anglicans. The building ceased to be a place of worship in 1956. (*Ray Davies*)

In 1952 the opening of the Assizes was marked with a service at St Mary's parish church followed by a parade down the High Street and into King Street, passing the National School before entering the courthouse. These were important occasions as can be seen by the formal lines of the children in the playground of the National School, now King Street car park. The little girl second from the end on the bottom right of the photograph is impressed by the splendour and importance of the bewigged and robed figure of the judge as she appears to be saluting. (*Quentin Dodd*)

This 1912 Certificate of Merit awarded to Harriet Roberts for 'Regular and Punctual
Attendance, combined with Diligence in School Work' recorded the fact she made 342
attendances out of a possible 343. The certificate is wonderfully decorated and is a testament
to the days when the pupils receiving them treasured such documents. *(Olwen Richardson)*

12

Transport

The Railway Station, Mold

Mold station stood on the Chester to Holyhead branch line, known as the Mold Railway. It was opened in 1849 and stretched from the Mold Junction (Saltney Ferry) and was ten miles in length. In 1869, a sixteen-mile extension from Mold to Denbigh, the Mold–Denbigh Railway, was completed and an 1876 trade directory describes the station as being part of the London and North Western Railway, though sadly, it finally closed to passenger traffic in 1962. *(Rhiannon Griffiths)*

I am of the generation old enough to remember when trainspotting was the norm for boys and not the preserve of enthusiasts we would today call 'anoraks'. Looking at this 1950s picture, I'm sure many of us can remember the smell of these wonderful pieces of engineering which still bring nostalgic tears of joy to steam enthusiasts, although I have to admit I am no longer one of their number. *(Ray Davies)*

With the demise of passenger trains courtesy of Dr Beeching, many stations became redundant, and in the case of Mold the station became a builder's yard. I remember using its services shortly after I arrived in Mold in 1983. A number of the smaller stations have been converted into houses of character, while others have been demolished. The location of Mold station now houses a Tesco superstore, while part of the old track line is another of Mold's car parks. *(Ray Davies)*

Above: In those long lost days of transport synchronisation, and long before I became eligible for a bus pass, bus stations were normally adjacent to the railway station and looking down Chester Street, we can see the old bus station on the left and the parcel office on the right. The parcel office has since disappeared and the bus shelter is now a shop catering to the modern trend of cladding our floors with laminate. *(Ray Davies)*

Right: An 1876 trade directory lists the stationmaster of Llong, on the Chester, Mold and Denbigh line of the London and North Western Railway, as Samuel Eaton. Pictured in 1954, all that remains is the old station and the two road crossing gates. The railway served the industry that abounded in the area, including three collieries called Hop, Skip and Jump. *(R. Casserley)*

The station has been converted into a private house and, apart from the busy road running alongside the small number of houses, the area is now agricultural. Today's visitor would be hard pressed to imagine industrial workers using the maze of footpaths on their way to Llong and Padeswood. An early mention of Llong is made during the English Civil Wars where a Royalist Captain Denys Llong of Llong was named in a revolt of 1659. *(Eric Keen)*

The provision of public transport in days past was paramount, as private motorcars were few and far between and were limited to the wealthier members of society. Pictured is a London & North Western Railway omnibus that plied its trade between Connah's Quay and Mold, via Flint and Northop. Among the later bus companies were Crosville and the Llanarmon-based E.G. Peters Motor Services, and today's residents will all know New Street-based Eagles and Crawford. *(Ray Davies)*

Brooke's Brothers coaches were a common sight in the early 1900s and pictured here are two coaches parked on the lower part of Mold High Street. The open-top buses clearly did not offer passengers a lot of protection during inclement weather. Apart from the dress standard of the time it is also worth noting the registration number, as DM, signifying the vehicle was registered in Flintshire. The vehicle licensing office was situated in Hall Fields. *(Ray Davies)*

While an accurate date for this photograph is not known, a new organ was installed in St Mary's parish church in 1923 therefore it is reasonable to assume that the raffle was part of the fundraising activity for that provision. The car appears to have been donated by Tom James of Mold and a silent film of the car and those involved is in the possession of the Mold and District Civic Society. *(Ray Davies)*

I am not sure whether this is the ladies' motorcycle named as the second prize in
the Mold Church Organ Fund raffle, but from the number plate, we know that it was
registered in Flintshire. For the motorcycle enthusiast, the author is reliably informed
that it is a Scott motorcycle with a water-cooled two-stroke engine with belt drive, sloping
cylinder and calliper brakes. *(Ray Davies)*

Pictured on his hand-built Titan agricultural tractor is Henry George Harley (1883–1975)
who was responsible for the founding of the legendary Harley's garage. Born the son of a
cowman at Ty Draw farm, he was educated at the Gwysaney Estate School on the Denbigh
road. After leaving school at the age of twelve, his first job was cutting thistles on the
estate before becoming a liveried groom for Edwards the vet. When the horse was finally
replaced by a motor vehicle, his lifelong interest in cars began. *(Ray Davies)*

The first Harley's garage started after the First World War in the Dolphin station yard before moving to Daniel Powell's (grocer) yard and then onto the current premises in Chester Street. This 1924 photograph of the original Chester Street premises shows the founder, just visible at the open doorway, and at that time, petrol cost 1s per gallon. The business was eventually taken over by one of his sons, Trevor, who, despite being in his eighties, continued to run the business until his death in 2005. (*Ray Davies*)

As with many of our older towns, Mold was not designed to cater for the many heavy vehicles travelling to and from the various quarries, or indeed, for the increased volume of private vehicles. In the early 1990s a new bypass was in the process of being built, and this view towards Gwernymynydd, with the wall around the old county gaol on the right, shows the new road under construction. (*Eric Keen*)

Originally the road between Ruthin and Mold was called Clay Lane but has now been renamed Clayton Road. Here we see the road after a heavy snowfall in April 1998. Snow is not the only hazard this road has witnessed, as in 1758, the town was reprimanded for not filling in the ruts and in the 1760s, the landlord of the Dolphin Hotel appeared before the bench for dumping cartloads of dirt and filth onto the road. *(Eric Keen)*

In November 2000 Mold suffered major flooding, including the town centre, and the RNLI inshore lifeboats were fully employed in getting people back to dry land. This photograph taken from Chester Street shows the scene on the old railway line car park, and it was not a happy time for those motorists parked in the 'lake'. The buildings, from left to right, are the police station, Aldi supermarket, fire station, ambulance station, St David's Catholic Church and, high and dry, the old chapel. *(Peter Thomas)*

13

Market Day

As the town was part of a medieval marcher lordship, it is likely that Mold possessed a trading charter prior to it falling into 'decay' in the early sixteenth century. Indeed, the story associated with the death of the Mayor of Chester at Tower refers to him visiting Mold Market in the fifteenth century. In 1653 there were two annual fairs held on 20 July and 11 November. *(Ray Davies)*

Flintshire Record Office has probably one of the first of the modern charters granted to the town. Dated 14 December 1732, it grants the Lord of the Manor of Mold, Anthony Langley Swymer, a licence to hold a market each Wednesday and four fairs annually. The fairs were to be held on 22 July, 11 November (the Feast of St Martin), 10 March and the Wednesday immediately preceding Ascension Day. If the first three fell on a Sunday they were to be held on the following Monday. *(Ray Davies)*

The 1732 charter permitted 'the buying and selling of all kinds of fowl, meat, fish, fruits, grains, roots and herbs and other provisions and all other kinds of merchandise usually bought and sold at markets and fairs'. As can be seen in this photograph, the range of goods has changed over the years and while some foodstuffs are still sold, the goods now reflect the current demand, including videos, CD's, plants, replica sportswear and do-it-yourself tools. *(Ray Davies)*

The Mold Market Co. was formed in 1845 to demolish the old manorial Leet courthouse which still stood on the site of the Assembly Hall in the left foreground. The intention was to provide a permanent home for the butchers' shambles and traders' stalls that were erected in the street, and as a result, the Assembly Hall was built. Mold Local Board purchased the Cross Market for £2,500 in 1882 and it remained the town's only covered market until 1976. *(Glynn Morris)*

It is often forgotten that the town also has an indoor market that has had a number of homes. Among items for sale in the current stalls are wools, handbags, ladies' lingerie, greeting cards, lighting, sweets, fish and haberdashery. *(Glynn Morris)*

Above: In this 1980s photograph, taken from Compton House on the Cross, the traffic problem and risk to shoppers is only too evident. Clearly this hazard had to be eradicated. The banner across the road at the rear of the picture announces an event to be held in Mold. *(Ray Davies)*

Left: This picture, taken on a cloudy day in October 2000, shows how much more pleasant shopping has become with the absence of traffic in the lower part of the High Street. The picture is also an iconic view of Mold in that it captures the history of the town through Bailey Hill and St Mary's Church while reflecting the current dynamic life of a town I am proud to call home. *(Eric Keen)*

ACKNOWLEDGEMENTS

It is fitting that the acknowledgement page has two farewell pictures taken of a young Joan Tapper, with her sister Eileen and Miss Edwards in 1931 on the pond at her father's farm near Ysceifiog. Now in her late eighties, she and many like her have been my inspiration for getting involved in various community projects. To all those (too numerous to mention), who have either directly or indirectly contributed to this book, I owe a great debt of gratitude.

Those who provided photographs are listed throughout the book, and without their kind assistance, this would not have been possible.

Special thanks must go to Matilda Pearce at Sutton Publishing for her guidance and assistance; Ken Lloyd Gruffydd for his Welsh translation and helpful tips; Mold Town Council; Mold Town Library; Flintshire Reference Library at County Hall Complex; Flintshire Record Office at Hawarden; Chris Bithell and Rhiannon Griffiths for sharing their local knowledge and checking the accuracy of my efforts; the late Vic Harley for his encouragement, Judith Rowe for reminding me of the grammar I learnt at school all those years ago; and Eric Keen, for his boundless energy and willingness to go and take 'just one more photograph' at a moment's notice.

Last, but certainly not least, I undoubtedly owe the greatest debt to my friend Ray Davies who made available his extensive collection of photographs and postcards without hesitation, and despite being an octogenarian, he has shown great enthusiasm throughout. Perhaps it was only to stop him getting under his wife Grace's feet, but without him, I certainly could not have even contemplated this book.

Diolch yn fawr

Also by The History Press

Cardiff: A Centenary Celebration, 1905–2005
John O'Sullivan, ISBN 978 0 7509 4181 5, £12.99

❧

Cardiff's Vanished Docklands
Brian Lee, ISBN 978 0 7509 4424 3, £12.99

❧

Yesterday's Cardiff
Brian Lee, ISBN 978 0 7509 4616 2, £12.99

❧

A Century of Llandudno: Events, People & Places over the 20th Century
Jim Roberts, ISBN 978 0 7509 4936 1, £9.99

❧

The Mystery of Jack of Kent and the Fate of Owain Glyndwr
Alex Gibbon, ISBN 978 0 7509 3319 3, £18.99

❧

Roman & Early Medieval Wales
C.J. Arnold & Jeffrey L. Davies, ISBN 0978 0 7509 2174 9, £25

❧

Snowdonia: In and Around the National Park
Jim Roberts, ISBN 978 0 7509 2267 8, £9.99

❧

South Wales Murders
Bob Hinton, ISBN 978 0 7509 4809 8, £12.99

❧

Swansea at War
Sally Bowler, ISBN 978 0 7509 4464 9, £12.99

❧

When Wales Went to War, 1939–45
John O'Sullivan, ISBN 978 0 7509 3837 2, £12.99